Retirement Benefits and Teacher Retention

A Structural Modeling Approach

David Knapp, Kristine M. Brown, James Hosek,
Michael G. Mattock, Beth J. Asch

For more information on this publication, visit www.rand.org/t/RR1448

Library of Congress Cataloging-in-Publication Data
is available for this publication.

ISBN: 978-0-8330-9451-3

Published by the RAND Corporation, Santa Monica, Calif.
© Copyright 2016 RAND Corporation
RAND® is a registered trademark.

Cover Image: "Young Men Teacher," Fotolia, 1001color

Support RAND
Make a tax-deductible charitable contribution at
www.rand.org/giving/contribute

www.rand.org

Preface

Recently, many state governments have legislated reductions in teachers' retirement benefits for new and future employees as a means of addressing the large unfunded liabilities of their pension plans. However, there is little existing capacity to predict how these unprecedented pension reforms—and, more broadly, changes to teacher compensation—will affect teacher turnover and teacher experience mix, which, in turn, could affect the cost and efficacy of the public education system. Our research develops a modeling capability to begin filling that gap. We develop and estimate a stochastic dynamic programming model to analyze the relationship between compensation, including retirement benefits, and retention over the career of Chicago public school teachers. The structural modeling approach we use was first developed at the RAND Corporation for the purpose of studying the relationship between military compensation and the retention of military personnel and is called the dynamic retention model, or DRM. Although the peer-reviewed literature on teachers includes research on retirement benefits and the timing of retirement, the research does not model compensation and retention over the length of the career from entry to exit (into retirement or an alternative career), and it has limited capability to predict the effect of compensation and retirement benefit changes on retention. By comparison, the DRM is well suited to these tasks, and the DRM specification developed here for Chicago teachers fits their career retention profile well. Future work could apply the model to other school districts and states, develop costing capability to examine the retention effects and costs of alternative policy changes, and extend the data and analysis to include school and student characteristics and information on teacher effectiveness.

Contents

Figures

Tables

Summary

School districts recognize compensation as an important factor in teacher retention and retirement, but there is little existing capability to predict how changes in current compensation or retirement benefits alter teacher retention over a career and affect retirement decisions. The purpose of this research is to begin filling that gap. We develop a structural stochastic dynamic programming model that links teacher retention and compensation. The estimates of the structural model are informative about the relative importance of compensation and non-pecuniary factors in retention decisions, and the estimated model can be used to evaluate proposed changes to compensation policies. This structural approach was originally developed to study the retention of military personnel with respect to compensation and is known as the dynamic retention model (DRM). Military service and the military as an organization are distinctly different from teaching and schools, but there are similarities in the retention profiles of military personnel and teachers and in their compensation systems, suggesting the potential usefulness of the DRM for analyzing teacher retention. In addition, as an indication of its versatility, the DRM is being successfully adapted to the federal civil service workforce (Asch, Mattock, and Hosek, 2014a, 2014b).

The growing literature on teacher retention indicates that financial incentives from both current and deferred compensation (retirement benefits) are related to teacher retention in a school district and in the teaching profession more generally. However, the results from the existing literature cannot be readily used to predict the effect of alternative compensation policies on retention. This is the first study that estimates a structural model of teacher retention in a large school district. The structural modeling approach has a distinct advantage over other approaches because it permits quantitative assessments of the retention effects of compensation policies for which no data or limited data exist. With the estimated model, we can simulate the effect of changes to current and deferred compensation on teacher retention decisions over the career, from entry to exit or retirement.

Our analysis focuses on the retention of Chicago public school teachers, but the features of Chicago teachers' compensation are not atypical. Teacher salaries are determined through a collective bargaining process and follow a salary schedule based on years of experience and formal education. Teachers are also covered by a back-loaded defined benefit retirement plan, which creates particularly strong retention incentives as teachers approach the plan retirement age. These features of Chicago teachers' compensation are included in the DRM.

The DRM is an econometric model of retention behavior. In it, employees make retention decisions each year over their career with a given employer. The model assumes that these employees are rational and forward-looking, taking into account their expected future earnings from the employer (current and deferred), as well as their own preference for employment with that employer, and uncertainty about future events that could cause them to value their current service more or less, relative to their external opportunities. The DRM allows for heterogeneity in employees' permanent preferences or "taste" for employment with their current employer, relative to other employment options. This means that the model can accommodate variation across teachers with respect to their satisfaction with teaching in general, working in Chicago public schools in particular, and the (nonpecuniary) desirability of their alternative employment options.

We explored several extensions of this baseline model and found that a version incorporating an early-career preference for teaching in Chicago, in addition to the permanent taste for teaching in Chicago already included in the model, provided the best fit of teacher retention. The additional early-career taste is modeled to be the same for all Chicago hires and decreases as teachers gain experience in their first ten or so years of service in Chicago. Such downward adjustment in the taste for teaching early in the career is consistent with many candidate causes, such as a decrease in the personal satisfaction from teaching or an increase in duties related to administration, discipline, or reporting requirements that, while necessary, may take away from the nonpecuniary benefit of being a teacher. We are not able to pin down the specific drivers in this study, but the finding suggests that this deserves further research.

The model was estimated using personnel data, which allowed us to follow teachers over their careers in Chicago (1979–2012) and to observe their salaries, ages, and years of district service as of each year. The predicted retention profile fits the data well. The parameter estimates suggest that teachers enter teaching in Chicago with a high initial taste that decreases over the first ten or so years of teaching, and this is an important driver of the early-career attrition. There is also significant variation in the permanent taste for teaching. Teachers with higher permanent taste are more likely to stay, and the average taste of retained teachers increases with teacher experience once the decline in initial taste has run its course.

Using the estimated model, we simulate several hypothetical changes to Chicago teacher compensation. We find the largest changes to the retention profiles occur when current salaries are reduced and when the full retirement age is increased. Simulations suggest a permanent 3-percent reduction in salary results in significantly lower retention for early-career teachers in years one to five. An increase in the full retirement age leads to lower retention of mid-career teachers, but the retention of teachers who continue teaching beyond the full retirement age is higher given that teachers with lower taste tend to have left by the new full retirement age.

The estimated model implies that teacher retention decisions are sensitive to both current salary and retirement benefits. The analysis here has generated a baseline model that can be applied to states (including Illinois) and other school districts to better understand how reforms of teacher pensions or changes to salary schedules (e.g., performance-based vs. experience-based pay) affect teacher retention, and at what cost. This model can also be extended to include nonpecuniary factors that may affect teacher retention, such as a mentoring program for new teachers, and to explore selective retention by teacher effectiveness.

Acknowledgments

Funding for this study was provided by philanthropic contributions from RAND supporters and income from operations. We thank RAND Education, especially Darleen Opfer, Director of RAND Education, and Brian Stecher, for their support and encouragement at early stages of this work. We received helpful comments from Catherine Augustine of RAND Education and from our reviewers, Kathleen Mullen of RAND and Paco Martorell of the University of California at Davis. We thank Whitney Dudley, who provided research programming support. We are deeply grateful to the Illinois State Board of Education (ISBE), especially Megan Griffin and Tim Simmons for supplying the Illinois Teacher Service Record data. The findings of this study are our own and do not necessarily reflect those of ISBE or the Chicago Teachers' Pension Fund.

Abbreviations

CPI	consumer price index
CPS	Chicago Public Schools
COLA	cost-of-living adjustment
CTPF	Chicago Teachers' Pension Fund
CTU	Chicago Teachers Union
DRM	dynamic retention model
FAS	final average salary
ISAT	Illinois Standards Achievement Test
ISBE	Illinois State Board of Education
NTE	National Teachers Exam
RCT	randomized control trial
TSR	Illinois Teacher Service Record

CHAPTER ONE

Introduction

Policies that will significantly affect teacher compensation are rolling out across the country. In response to the large underfunded liabilities of teachers' pensions,[1] many state governments have legislated reductions in teachers' retirement benefits for new and future employees (Clark, 2012). These benefits are a substantial portion of teacher compensation, and changes to the level and timing of this compensation for teachers could alter turnover rates at different points along the career profile. Offsetting adjustments to other forms of compensation would then be required to maintain the status quo career profile (if desired) and, depending on their design, might do so less efficiently. At the same time, there is a growing push to improve the teaching workforce by shifting away from traditional experience- and education-based teacher salary schedules to salaries based on teacher effectiveness. Changes to retirement benefits may interact with and influence the effectiveness these salary reforms.

While the funding situation of teacher retirement systems has received considerable attention, less attention has been paid to how pension reforms—and, more broadly, changes to teacher compensation—affect teacher turnover and teacher experience mix. Our research develops a modeling capability to begin filling that gap.

---

[1]   Munnell and Aubry (2015) report that the aggregated expected liability of 150 state and local pension plans is $4.3 trillion, but these plans have the assets to cover only 74 percent of this liability, leaving $1.1 trillion (approximately 6,5 percent of the U.S. 2014 gross domestic product) unfunded. As a subset of state and local plans, many teacher pension systems are in poor health, and all but one were underfunded in 2014.

We develop a stochastic dynamic programming model to analyze the relationship between compensation, including retirement benefits, and retention over the career of Chicago public school teachers. The results of the model estimation indicate the relative importance of compensation and nonpecuniary factors in retention decisions. However, the distinct advantage of the structural modeling approach over other approaches is that the estimated model can be used to simulate the retention effects of counterfactual compensation policies for which no data or limited data exist.

As in other workforces, retention varies over the teacher career. Public school districts typically have the highest outflow of teachers at the beginning of a career, then low outflow in mid-career years, and higher outflow once the retirement eligibility date is reached. Relevant research suggests that 57 percent of new-entrant teachers remained at their school for three to five years, and 47 percent remained for six to ten years.[2] Turnover for teachers with more than ten years of experience is relatively low. For example, the continuation rate from 11 to 30 years of experience for teachers in Texas was 86.9 percent (Hanushek, Kain, and Rivkin, 2004).

Understanding how compensation affects retention is valuable because turnover is costly. Although there is a sorting process underlying turnover, in which individuals who do not fit well with an organization or who discover superior external opportunities will leave, it is important to recognize that the benefits of turnover come at a cost. According to a pilot study of five urban and rural school districts conducted by the National Commission on Teaching and America's Future (2007), the average cost of replacing a teacher, including recruiting, hiring, and training, was $17,872 for Chicago, the district studied in

---

[2]   Papay et al. (2015) studied teachers in 16 urban school districts and found that 55 percent left their district within five years. In addition, 70 percent of new entrants left their school within five years but remained in their district. Hanushek, Kain, and Rivkin (2004), using Texas data, found that 26 percent of teachers with zero to two years of experience left their school from one year to the next, as did 22 percent of teachers with three to five years of experience and 18 percent of teachers with six to ten years of experience. These percentages suggest that 57 percent of new-entrant teachers remained at their school for three to five years, and 47 percent remained for six to ten years.

this report (replacement costs were similar in Milwaukee and lower for rural districts). The total annual cost of turnover in the Chicago schools was estimated to be above $86 million per year.

The cost of turnover goes beyond the budgetary expense of replacing a teacher. Turnover can result in a lack of continuity in instruction, inadequate teacher expertise for making curriculum decisions, and fewer experienced teachers to serve as mentors (Loeb, Darling-Hammond, and Luczak (2005). The replacement of an experienced teacher by a novice implies a loss of human capital; experienced personnel who leave take with them knowledge about policies, procedures, tactics, and mentoring and leadership capability.

The literature on teachers is vast, and some of that literature has focused on teacher retention. However, as we discuss in Chapter Three, the literature is quite sparse in terms of models that support counterfactual—or "what if"—policy analysis of how pension reforms or other compensation changes affect teacher retention over the career. Such counterfactual policy analysis requires a structural modeling approach, but that approach has not been used in the past to analyze teacher retention.

The structural, stochastic dynamic programming model of teacher retention and compensation developed in our research permits counterfactual analyses, using data on the Chicago Public Schools system. The approach we use in this study, also known as the dynamic retention model (DRM), was first developed in the early 1980s to study the retention of military personnel. It has been used to inform policy by assessing the effects of proposed reforms of the military retirement system, bonuses and special pays, separation incentives, and annual pay and cost-of-living increases on personnel costs and military personnel retention. As an indication of its versatility, the DRM has been adapted to the federal civil service workforce (Asch, Mattock, and Hosek, 2014a, 2014b), even though federal civilian service and military service involve quite distinctive careers and external opportunities. Similarly, military service and the military as an organization are distinctly different from teaching and schools, but there are similarities suggesting the potential usefulness of the DRM for analyzing teacher retention. These similarities include similar retention patterns over the career, e.g., high early attrition, high mid-career and senior retention, and high turnover among retirement-eligible personnel. Another similarity is the use of a defined benefit retirement system and an experience-based pay table as a basis for computing current compensation.

The DRM provides a platform for addressing policy questions regarding teacher compensation and retention because, once estimated, the model can be used to conduct policy simulations showing the effect of compensation changes on retention and their cost. These questions could include, to what extent would higher teacher pay, or a continuation bonus, decrease turnover, and how much would it cost? And how would pension reforms that change the benefit formula or mandate higher employee contributions affect retention over a career, as well as cost?

Although most teacher retirement benefits are defined benefit plans, it may be worthwhile for school districts to consider a blended plan. The military, having used much the same defined benefit plan since 1947, may switch to a blended plan with both a defined benefit and a defined contribution.[3] A blended plan might be attractive to districts and teachers for similar reasons, and applying the DRM to teacher retention is a step toward building the capability to explore this possibility. Introducing a blended system or altering a current pension system to enable buyouts may help to decrease the unfunded liability, but analysis is needed to give a specific estimate of the potential decrease. Though not done here, the DRM approach has the potential to explore these options.

Developing a DRM of teacher retention required several steps. First, it required gathering information on teacher pension systems and teacher careers so that we can incorporate key institutional features

---

[3]   In the current Congress, the House and Senate Armed Services Committees have produced bills with blended plans—a major retirement reform. The plans allow incumbent service members to opt into the blended plan but otherwise keeps them under the current plan and places new entrants under the blended plan. Analysis with the DRM has shown how a blended plan can be beneficial to service members, offer military services greater flexibility in managing personnel, and reduce cost (Asch, Hosek, and Mattock, 2014; Asch, Mattock, and Hosek, 2015).

into the model. The second key step was developing new code for the DRM that reflects the institutional features of teacher retirement compensation and estimating teacher pay schedules and external earnings opportunities to include in the model. This step also involved developing new code enabling the model to be estimated with data on entering cohorts of teachers combined with data on teachers present in a given year. Third, longitudinal data on teacher retention had to be obtained to estimate the model. Finally, the model was estimated and used to conduct policy simulations to illustrate its capability.

This report documents these steps and our key findings. The following two chapters describe the Chicago teacher pension system and discuss literature related to teacher retention. We then describe the DRM and the Chicago teacher data and, in Chapters Six and Seven, present the parameter estimates and describe the policy simulations we have done. The final chapter offers our assessment of the findings and outlines possible future work.

CHAPTER TWO

Overview of the Chicago Teachers' Employment Context

This chapter provides an overview of Chicago teachers' current and deferred compensation and highlights other features of the Chicago Public Schools (CPS) employment context that may affect teacher retention. Our study focuses on the effect of wages and pension benefits on the teacher retention profile. Other aspects of compensation, such as health insurance, are omitted from our analysis. However, in Chapter Six we discuss how these other factors relate to the interpretation of our results.

Compensation and Work Rules While Employed

Teachers in Chicago are members of the Chicago Teachers Union (CTU). Compensation and many aspects of working conditions are negotiated between the Chicago Board of Education and CTU and codified in a collective bargaining agreement.[1] As in many unionized school districts, salaries are determined by a pay table and are closely tied to position, teaching experience in the school district, and formal education or training. Teachers who take on extra duties may earn more than teachers with similar experience and education, but otherwise there is little variation in earnings. CPS also offers a stan-

---

[1] The most recent collective bargaining agreement between the Board of Education of the City of Chicago and Chicago Teachers Union Local 1, American Federation of Teachers, AFL-CIO, was entered into on October 24, 2012, and retroactively effective from July 1, 2012, to June 30, 2015. At the time of writing, a new contract had not been signed.

dard array of benefits, including employer-sponsored health insurance and paid sick leave. Historically, CPS has not offered performance pay, and the negotiated wage schedule does not offer any flexibility at the individual level. This prevents individual-targeted retention policies, such as the matching of outside employment offers. It also prevents rapid response to changing external labor market conditions overall or in particular fields, such as an increase in demand for those with science, technology, engineering, and math backgrounds. The result is that there may be heterogeneous retention by teacher quality or specialization. The compensation system is also a barrier to school-specific retention policies, so variation in working conditions, including student backgrounds and infrastructure quality, may also lead to heterogeneous retention by school assignment.

CPS also has a fairly generous leave policy for tenured teachers.[2] A teacher who returns from an approved temporary absence—for example, paternity/maternity leave—after no more than one year is guaranteed the option to return to his or her preleave position. A teacher who returns from an approved absence within four years is eligible for immediate assignment, though he or she is not guaranteed to be placed in the same position or school. This flexibility and job security is likely to be valued by teachers as part of the compensation and benefits package, which may contribute to retention. In addition, this temporary leave policy allows teachers to incur fewer costs by returning to employment in CPS following a break in teaching versus seeking employment outside CPS, reducing the likelihood of permanent separation.

Not all exits from CPS are the teacher's choice; involuntary separations occur due to school closures, budgetary reasons, or cause. Tenure and seniority in CPS generally afford teachers greater employment security, so they are less likely to exit CPS involuntarily. However, this link was weakened recently, and performance has become a more important determinant of job security, as discussed at the end of this chapter. In addition, it is not uncommon for CPS to lay off a large

---

[2] Teachers with three years of service with satisfactory performance reviews are granted tenure.

number of teachers at the beginning of the summer before the district budget has been set. Even though the majority of the teachers are recalled or reemployed before the school year begins, this practice creates significant uncertainty, especially among untenured and less experienced teachers. As a result, teachers may be more likely to seek and secure alternative employment early in their careers.

Defined Benefit Retirement Plan

Chicago teachers and administrators are covered by the Chicago Teachers' Pension Fund (CTPF), a defined benefit pension system. Established in 1895 by the State of Illinois legislature, CTPF was in good financial standing for much of its history, though its funding level has now fallen to 50 percent of its liabilities. CPS teachers opted out of Social Security and therefore do not receive Social Security credits while working in the Chicago public schools. CTPF also offers retiree health insurance, and teachers have participated in Medicare since 1986.

Chicago teachers in our period of study are covered by CTPF Tier 1 retirement plan. [3] This defined benefit pension plan has the features typical of most teachers' pensions in the United States (Hansen, 2010) and has similarities with the defined benefit plans of government employees and military personnel. The details of the retirement plan for the period under study are described later and summarized in Table 2.1.

---

[3]   Teachers hired on or after January 1, 2011, are in Tier 2 of the CTPF.

Table 2.1
Overview of the CTPF Defined Benefit Retirement Plan

Plan Feature	Tier 1 (Hired Before January 1, 2011)		Tier 2 (Hired on/After January 1, 2011)
	Service Earned Before July 1, 1998	Service Earned After July 1, 1998	
Employee contribution rate	8% of salary each year	9% of salary	9% of salary
Paid by employee	1% of salary each year	2% of salary each year	2% of salary each year
Paid by employer	7% of salary each year	7% of salary each year	7% of salary each year
Vesting service requirement	5 years		10 years
Benefit multiplier	1.67% for years of service 1–10 1.90% for years of service 11–20 2.10% for years of service 21–30 2.30% for years of service 31+	2.20% for all years of service	2.20% for all years of service
Max. retirement benefit	75% of final average salary		75% of final average salary
Normal retirement age	Age 55 with 33.95 or more years of service, or Age 60 with at least 20 years of service, or Age 62 with at least 5 years of service		67 with at least 10 years of service
Early retirement age	Age 55 with at least 20 years of service		62 with at least 10 years of service
Early retirement benefit reduction	Benefit is reduced by 6% for each year below age 60 or 33.95 years of service		Benefit is reduced by 6% for each year below age 67

Table 2.1—Continued

Plan Feature	Tier 1 (Hired Before January 1, 2011)	Tier 2 (Hired on/After January 1, 2011)
Final average salary	Average of salary for 4 highest consecutive earnings years, of most recent 10 years of service	Average of salary for 8 highest consecutive earnings years, of most recent 10 years of service
Pensionable earnings cap	None	Yes ($111,571.63 in 2015)
Cost of living adjustment	3% compounded annually beginning at the later of 1 year after retirement or age 61	Lesser of 3% or one-half of consumer price index (CPI), calculated on initial pension amount
Spouse survivor benefit	50% of retirement benefit	66 2/3% of retirement benefit (or earned annuity)

SOURCE: Chicago Teachers' Pension Fund, "Your CTPF Pension," undated.

Nine percent of a teacher's salary for each creditable year of service must be contributed to his or her pension while working.[4,5] CPS contributed 7 percent of salary on behalf of teachers during the time period we study, leaving the remainder, 2 percent, to be paid directly from the teacher's salary.[6] The portion paid by CPS is determined during contract negotiations and included in the collective bargaining agreement between the CPS Board and the CTU.

Teachers vest in CTPF Tier 1 after five years of service in CPS. Vesting makes them eligible to receive a retirement benefit, and the benefit is paid as a lifetime annuity. The CTPF normal retirement age decreases as years of service increase. A teacher with 33.95 years of service is eligible to retire with full benefits as early as age 55, while a teacher with at least 20 years of service can retire at 60, and a vested teacher with fewer than 20 years of service may not begin receiving pension income until age 62. At the normal retirement age, teachers are eligible for immediate receipt of the "full" retirement benefit, conditional on separation from employment in CPS. However, retirement from CPS does not imply retirement from the labor force. Retired CPS teachers may earn income by working in other school districts or in nonteaching professions while simultaneously collecting their CPS pension benefits.

The CTPF full benefit calculation follows the standard structure found in most defined benefit pensions. It is not explicitly tied to the contributions but is rather calculated as a fraction of each teacher's

---

[4]   This was 8 percent as of July 1, 1971, 9 percent as of July 1, 1998.

[5]   One year of service credit is received for a year in which the teacher was employed and received salary for 170 days or more. Partial-year credit is given when employment is for less than 170 days (Teachers' Retirement System of the State of Illinois, 2015a).

[6]   For example, suppose the teacher's monthly salary schedule amount was $5,000, and the Board paid 7 percent of salary to CTPF. Creditable earnings from the perspective of CTPF would be computed as $5,000/(1 − 0.07) = $5,376. The amount remitted to CTPF would be 0.09 × $5,376 = $484, which is nontaxable. The contribution paid by the Board is $376, and the contribution paid by the teacher is $108. Taxable earnings are $5,376 − $484 = $4,892. Because the entire 9 percent is excluded from the member's taxable income, it is treated as an employer contribution under the Internal Revenue Code and therefore meets the Illinois mandate that the employer pick up the entire 9 percent, regardless of who actually pays it (Teachers' Retirement System of the State of Illinois, 2015c).

average salary. The full benefit, B, is calculated as $M \times YOS \times FAS$, where M is the pension multiplier, YOS is the total number of covered years of service in CPS, and FAS is the teacher's "final average salary." The pension multiplier (M) was stepped by years of service before 1998 and has been 2.2 percent since 1998 (see Table 2.1). Together, the multiplier and years of service determine the fraction of the teacher's salary received as a retirement benefit, commonly referred to as the replacement rate. For example, under the 2.2-percent multiplier, a teacher with 20 years of service who has reached the normal retirement age of 60 will receive a retirement benefit equal to 44 percent (20 × 2.2 percent) of her final average salary. CTPF calculates the final average salary for Tier 1 teachers as the average of the four highest consecutive years of earnings within the most recent ten years of service; this is the last four years of earnings for most teachers.

The final average salary is the nominal average salary. For teachers retiring at the end of their work life, nominal average salary is typically only a few percentage points less than if the salary were adjusted for inflation to bring it to current-year dollars. However, the lack of an inflation adjustment makes a large difference to a teacher who leaves CPS after ten years of service at age 35 and claims CPS retirement benefits at age 62. At an annual average inflation rate of 2 percent, each dollar of FAS as of age 35 would have a real value at age 62 of $0.58—more than a 40 percent decrease in real value. This loss from inflation would be avoided if the teacher remained in CPS until normal retirement age.

A teacher with at least 20 years of service may retire (or claim) early, between ages 55 and 60, with a reduced benefit. But each year short of normal retirement age decreases the annual full retirement benefit by 6 percent. A teacher with 30.95 years of service can retire at age 57 instead of age 60 but with 18 percent less, or 0.82 of the normal-age benefit. An added wrinkle is that the normal retirement age changes based on years of service. Therefore, a similar 57-year-old teacher but with 31.95 years of service would have her benefit reduced by only 12 percent, because she would be eligible for a full pension with only two more years of service. Importantly, the benefit reduction is permanent. Teachers retiring before July 1, 2000, could retire early without a benefit reduction if they and CPS paid a fee to CTPF (Appendix A).

Teachers also have opportunities to increase their retirement benefits through the purchase of creditable years of service. Unused sick leave can be converted to service credits. The amount that can be converted is currently capped at 244 days, equivalent to 1.4 years of service. Teachers can buy creditable service for time spent on approved leave—e.g., maternity/paternity leave. The current maximum service purchase allowed for unpaid approved leaves of absence is 36 months. Appendix A describes these and additional service purchase options.

Once retirement benefits begin, they are adjusted for inflation. The annual cost of living adjustment (COLA) for CTPF Tier 1 teachers is 3 percent. The COLA starts one year after retirement, or at age 61, whichever is later. The COLAs are compounded.

Summarizing, the key aspects of retirement wealth accumulation in the CPTF include vesting after five years of service, eligibility to receive full retirement benefits at age 55 with 34 years of service, or age 60 with 20 or more years of service, or at age 62 with less than 20 years of service, and early retirement is possible with some benefit reduction. Benefit amount is determined by a typical defined benefit formula, $B = M \times YOS \times FAS$, and final average salary is stated in nominal terms as of the years it was earned. Retirement benefits, when received, have an annual COLA of 3 percent.

Retention Incentives of CTPF Retirement Benefits

In this section, we present an example of CTPF retirement benefits. Key factors in the teacher's accumulation of retirement benefit wealth are (1) vesting at the completion of five years of service; the teacher has no retirement wealth until vesting; (2) fairly steady increase in benefit amount as a result of pay increases, especially during the first 20 years of service; (3) a bump up in retirement wealth upon completing 20 years of service, at which point the normal retirement age for full benefits decreases from 62 to 60; (4) another bump up upon the completion of 34 years of service (more precisely, 33.95 years), at which point the retirement benefit multiplier reaches its maximum of 75 percent. A teacher who begins in CPS at age 22 will reach 34 years of service at age 55 and is eligible to retire at that age. Beyond this point, accrual becomes negative for this teacher, because the small increment in benefit amount from the increase in FAS from an additional year of work does not offset the loss of one year of benefits. (5) Teachers can retire early, before their normal retirement age of 60 or 55, but at a penalty of 6 percent of their benefit for each year less than their normal retirement age. (6) Benefits are adjusted by COLA starting one year after the teacher reaches normal retirement age. For teachers who vest but leave CPS before the normal retirement age, there is no COLA to their FAS prior to one year after normal retirement age.

Table 2.2 presents an example of the accumulation of retirement wealth over a teacher's career. The earnings in the example are based on the annual earnings for a CPS teacher in our sample used in estimating the DRM. The left-hand columns show age, years of service, and annual earnings in constant (inflation-adjusted) dollars. FAS is an average of the four most recent years of earnings, as they are the highest consecutive four years. The deflator column indicates the purchasing power at age 55 of a current-age dollar. This is relevant because benefits are based on FAS, and they are not adjusted to keep pace with inflation, so a dollar has a lower real value at retirement than it does in the current year. The next column, annual retirement benefit in constant dollars, applies the deflator in calculating the value of the benefit. Age 55 is used as the base year for the deflator because, in this example, the teacher will have 34 years of service at age 55 and have the maximum multiplier at that time. The assumed age of retirement follows the benefit eligibility rules of CTPF and so is age 62 once a teacher has vested (has more than five years of service) and decreases to age 60 when the teacher has 20 years of service. For some teachers, the age that optimizes retirement wealth may be early, i.e., before age 60 and as early as age 55, the youngest allowable age to draw benefits. In the example, a teacher with 32 years of service at age 53 who is considering leaving teaching at that point will do better by claiming retirement benefits at age 55 rather than age 60, where "better" means a higher present discounted value of retirement wealth at age 53. The table also shows

Table 2.2
CTPF Retirement Wealth and Present Discounted Value of Retirement Wealth: Example

Age	Years of Service	Annual Earnings in Constant Dollars	Final Average Salary (FAS)	Deflator (Age 55 = 1.00)	Annual Retirement Benefit in Constant Dollars (B)	Normal Age of Retirement	Retirement Wealth as of Normal Age of Retirement	Retirement Age Maximizing Retirement Wealth Discounted to Current Age	Retirement Wealth Discounted to Current Age
22	1	45,254		0.520	0				0
23	2	48,236		0.531	0				0
24	3	51,218		0.541	0				0
25	4	54,200		0.552	0				0
26	5	57,182		0.563	0				0
27	6	58,977	55,394	0.574	4,200	62	61,115	62	7,951
28	7	60,773	57,783	0.586	5,213	62	75,863	62	10,462
29	8	62,568	59,875	0.598	6,297	62	91,636	62	13,396
30	9	64,363	61,670	0.610	7,443	62	108,306	62	16,783
31	10	66,158	63,466	0.622	8,681	62	126,320	62	20,749
32	11	66,856	64,986	0.634	9,973	62	145,127	62	25,268
33	12	67,555	66,233	0.647	11,310	62	164,585	62	30,375

Table 2.2—Continued

Age	Years of Service	Annual Earnings in Constant Dollars	Final Average Salary (FAS)	Deflator (Age 55 = 1.00)	Annual Retirement Benefit in Constant Dollars (B)	Normal Age of Retirement	Retirement Wealth as of Normal Age of Retirement	Retirement Age Maximizing Retirement Wealth Discounted to Current Age	Retirement Wealth Discounted to Current Age
34	13	68,253	67,205	0.660	12,681	62	184,536	62	36,101
35	14	68,951	67,904	0.673	14,075	62	204,812	62	42,471
36	15	71,293	69,013	0.686	15,633	62	227,486	62	50,004
37	16	71,802	70,075	0.700	17,270	62	251,313	62	58,556
38	17	72,311	71,089	0.714	18,988	62	276,303	62	68,241
39	18	72,819	72,056	0.728	20,786	62	302,468	62	79,185
40	19	73,328	72,565	0.743	22,537	62	327,956	62	91,009
41	20	73,632	73,023	0.758	24,350	62	369,254	62	122,043
42	21	73,996	73,444	0.773	26,230	60	397,752	60	139,350
43	22	74,359	73,829	0.788	28,175	60	427,254	60	158,667
44	23	74,722	74,177	0.804	30,187	60	457,759	60	180,195
45	24	75,085	74,540	0.820	32,287	60	489,600	60	204,293
46	25	74,566	74,683	0.837	34,370	60	521,196	60	230,526

Table 2.2—Continued

Age	Years of Service	Annual Earnings in Constant Dollars	Final Average Salary (FAS)	Deflator (Age 55 = 1.00)	Annual Retirement Benefit in Constant Dollars (B)	Normal Age of Retirement	Retirement Wealth as of Normal Age of Retirement	Retirement Age Maximizing Retirement Wealth Discounted to Current Age	Retirement Wealth Discounted to Current Age
47	26	74,666	74,760	0.853	36,498	60	553,454	60	259,481
48	27	74,766	74,771	0.871	38,665	60	586,322	60	291,384
49	28	74,866	74,716	0.888	40,869	60	619,745	55	341,790
50	29	74,966	74,816	0.906	43,233	60	655,593	55	410,965
51	30	75,066	74,916	0.924	45,679	60	692,688	55	489,925
52	31	75,166	75,016	0.942	48,210	60	731,068	55	579,769
53	32	75,266	75,116	0.961	50,828	60	770,770	55	681,706
54	33	75,366	75,216	0.980	53,536	60	811,833	55	797,058
55	34	75,466	75,316	1.000	56,337	55	927,278	55	927,278
56	35	75,566	75,416	1.020	57,694	56	879,735	56	879,735
57	36	75,666	75,516	1.040	58,925	57	825,006	57	825,006
58	37	75,766	75,616	1.061	60,184	58	765,763	58	765,763
59	38	75,866	75,716	1.082	61,468	59	701,587	59	701,587

Table 2.2—Continued

Age	Years of Service	Annual Earnings in Constant Dollars	Final Average Salary (FAS)	Deflator (Age 55 = 1.00)	Annual Retirement Benefit in Constant Dollars (B)	Normal Age of Retirement	Retirement Wealth as of Normal Age of Retirement	Retirement Age Maximizing Retirement Wealth Discounted to Current Age	Retirement Wealth Discounted to Current Age
60	39	75,966	75,816	1.104	62,781	60	632,192	60	632,192
61	40	76,066	75,916	1.126	64,121	61	557,277	61	557,277
62	41	76,166	76,016	1.149	65,489	62	476,524	62	476,524

retirement ages beyond age 55; here, the final average salary increases slightly with age, but the multiplier is constant—the maximum of 75 percent is reached at age 55—and each year of work after 55 comes at the cost of one year of benefits forgone.

The column "retirement wealth as of normal age of retirement" is the present discounted value of the retirement benefit stream starting from the normal age of retirement to age 85, the assumed end of life. Discounting is done at a personal discount rate of 6 percent. Retirement wealth at the normal retirement age increases steadily until reaching its maximum at age 55, then decreases. The decrease occurs because the increase in final average salary is not fast enough to overcome the negative effects of one year of benefits forgone and one less year to draw benefits.

The final column makes an important connection to the DRM in two ways. In the DRM, retirement benefits payable in future years are, in effect, discounted to the current year of the teacher's retention decision. As the table shows, if a 41-year-old teacher with 20 years of service were to leave teaching and have no further retirement accumulation, that teacher's CTPF retirement wealth would be $369,254 at age 60 (in inflation-adjusted dollars), the normal retirement age. But the present discounted value of that wealth would be much less, $122,043. The DRM also assumes optimizing behavior, and as the second-to-right column shows, teachers aged 49 to 54 and with 28 to 33 years of service would choose to claim benefits at age 55 instead of at the normal age of 60.

Figure 2.1, based on the table, illustrates the present discounted value of retirement wealth to current age, assuming benefits are claimed when the present discounted value is highest.

An implication of the example is that the present discounted value of retirement wealth is relatively small—about $21,000 in the tenth year of teaching, and $50,000 in the 15th year of teaching. Therefore, the influence of retirement benefits on teacher retention is likely to be small in early-career years. The influence should be greater among teachers with more experience. The present discounted value of retirement wealth increases rapidly after age 40 or so in this example, because of increases in two elements of the retirement benefit formula—years

Figure 2.1
Present Discounted Value of Retirement Wealth, by Age

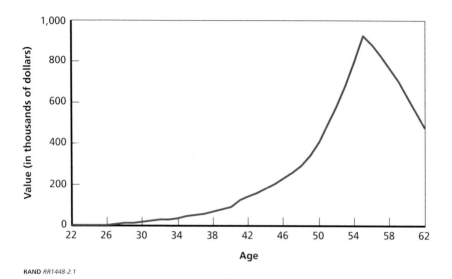

RAND *RR1448-2.1*

of service and final average salary—and because retirement benefits are discounted for fewer years as the retirement age approaches. Also, the present discounted values of retirement wealth in the example depend on the personal discount rate, assumed to be 6 percent. If the rate were higher, the values would be lower.

Recent Trends in the CPS Employment Context

CPS has undergone governance changes and shifts in school structure since the 1980s. Following the turmoil and contentious labor relations of the late 1980s, including a 19-day teacher strike in 1987, the Chicago School Reform Act was passed, creating a new local school council governing system.[7] Governance was restructured again in 1995 when the Illinois legislature awarded the mayor of Chicago, then Richard M. Daley, the authority to appoint a CPS management team, including a

---

[7]   Chicago Public Schools, 2015b.

CEO. The legislation also curtailed rights of the CTU to bargain over key working conditions. Under the leadership of CEO Arne Duncan (2001–2009), more than 40 poorly performing and underattended schools closed, and over a dozen were designated for turnaround. Many turnaround schools were managed by private organizations following the school action, and many new charter schools opened during this period. School closures, turnarounds, and the expansion of charter schools continued following Duncan's term as CEO. In 2012–2013, 47 Chicago schools were closed, the largest number closed in a single year by any district in the nation at that time (de la Torre et al., 2015). As of August 2014, Chicago had 131 charter schools, and nearly 40 percent of high schools in the district were charter schools.[8]

District school closures and turnarounds affect the employment of teachers and their working conditions. They displace the leadership and the teaching staff at the designated schools. Teachers in schools that are closed can be employed in their students' new assigned school if there is an appropriate vacancy, and if their performance ratings were high in the previous year. Teachers in turnaround schools are usually required to reapply for their teaching positions, but the likelihood of being rehired has not been high. A study of 36 school turnarounds in Chicago found that only five schools reported retaining or rehiring more than 50 percent of the original teaching staff (de la Torre et al., 2013). Following displacement by school action, the onus is on the teacher to secure a new position within the district.[9]

At the same time, the number of charter schools in Chicago has expanded, further altering the teaching landscape in the district. Chi-

---

[8]   Authors' calculations using publicly available district statistics from Chicago Public Schools, 2015a.

[9]   Per the 2012–2015 CTU contract, tenured teachers affected by school closure may transfer to the receiving school if their most recent rating is in the top two performance categories. Tenured teachers laid off due to school actions are assigned to the reassigned teacher pool for five school months, during which time they will receive full pay and benefits and priority in being assigned as a substitute teacher. At the end of five months, the teacher will be assigned to the substitute teacher cadre for a period of five months with cadre pay and benefits. At the end of that time, the teacher will be laid off and separated from employment if a permanent position has not been found. Alternatively, a displaced teacher may choose to resign and receive three months of pay, rather than enter the reassignment pool (CTU, undated[b]).

cago charter schools are public schools but are not obligated to negoti-ate with the CTU or bound by the CTU contract. Thus, teachers in charter schools do not necessarily receive the same salaries, have the same employment protections, or face the same working conditions as teachers in the traditional public schools, though they are covered by the same retirement system. The increase in charter schools may have increased the variation in teacher pay within CPS. Teachers at 12 Chicago charter schools have organized under the Chicago Alliance of Charter Teachers and Staff, which affiliated with the American Federa-tion of Teachers, like CTU.[10]

The district had 682 schools and a total of 396,641 students in 2013–2014, the latest available school data at the time of writing. This includes 65,489 English language learner (ELL) students and 51,850 students with individualized education programs (IEPs). There were 23,319 average total teachers (full-time equivalent [FTE]). Revenue per student was $14,294, and expenditure per student was $14,246 in 2011–2012, the latest available fiscal data.[11]

Following the passage of the No Child Left Behind Act in 2001, school districts have increasingly focused on assessment of student learning. CPS appears to have made progress in raising student scores on standardized tests since 2000.[12] Because research indicates that

---

[10]   Chicago Alliance of Charter Teachers and Staff, undated.

[11]   Institute of Education Sciences, National Center for Education Statistics, undated.

[12]   The percentage of students with a composite score meeting or exceeding the Illinois State Board of Education (ISBE) 2013 cut score doubled between 2001 and 2014, rising from 23.4 percent to 52.5 percent. The percentage of students in the warning range fell from 32.8 percent to 9.6 percent. The percentages are all relative to the 2013 ISBE cut score. The ISBE also reports these percentages relative to current-year cut scores (see ISBE, undated). For CPS the percentage meeting or exceeding the current-year cut score increased from 2000–2001 to 2008–2009, but the increase is not as fast as the increase based on the 2013 cut score, which suggests that the cut score was increasing relative to the Illinois Standards Achieve-ment Test (ISAT) scores. The percentage then decreased to 2012–2013, which suggests a faster increase in the current-year cut score in this period and/or a slower increase in ISAT scores. Chicago's increase followed by a decrease may be compared with the statewide ISAT meeting-or-exceeding percentages. They show a steady increase from 2001 to 2007 followed by a slight increase from 2007 to 2012 (authors' tabulations of CPS ISAT percentages and rc-trend-data02-14 from ISBE, undated).

working conditions are a factor in teacher retention (see the following chapter), teachers who remained in or joined CPS during this period may have benefited from improved working conditions and enjoyed greater satisfaction from their accomplishment in raising student achievement.

CHAPTER THREE

Insights from the Teacher Retention Literature

Although our research focuses on the relationship between teacher compensation and retention over a career, the literature is a rich source of information about a range a factors that affect teacher retention. The purpose of the literature review is to provide an awareness of these factors and their effects; even though they are not part of our data and model, they can help us understand the context in which teachers make their retention decisions and may help us interpret our results. We discuss teacher compensation, including state pension plans and pay and their effects on retention. We then discuss articles on noncompensation school attributes that may affect retention, including student and school characteristics and mentoring programs, and the incentives for teachers to change schools within districts. Finally, we address the relationship between teacher turnover and teacher effectiveness.

Retirement Plan Incentives and Their Effect on Teacher Retention

There has been significant growth in the research on teachers' retirement plans due both to the underfunding of teacher retirement plans (Clark, 2012) and to the increased focus on the role of teachers in education reforms. The research universally concludes that teachers' defined benefit retirement plans have particularly strong financial incentives tied to timing of exit from teaching. Costrell and Podgursky (2009) examine the annual accrual of pension wealth in six large teacher retirement systems—Ohio, Arkansas, California, Massachusetts, Missouri, and Texas—for a stylized teacher that enters teaching at age 25 and teaches continuously until exiting permanently. In all cases, teachers face sharply nonlinear pension wealth accrual schedules that provide large financial incentives to continue working to a specific age or for a certain number of years in the system. Beyond the age and years of service combination required to obtain the full benefit, the incentive to continue working falls off dramatically. For example, a teacher who has worked for 24 years in Arkansas will gain five times her salary in pension wealth if she stays just one more year to 25 years of service. This sharp accrual pattern is not atypical. More generally, the structure of the retirement benefit plan dictates these incentives, and teachers who are forward-looking can anticipate the expected gain in retirement wealth from longer retention conditional on the incentives.

Several studies, using different approaches, examined the relationship between the permanent financial incentives embedded in the teachers' defined benefit pension and their retirement behavior.[1] Overall, these studies demonstrate that the retirement timing of teachers aligns with the financial incentives of their pension plans. Teachers are less likely to retire when the increase in retirement benefits from additional years of service is large and are more likely to retire when the accrual of pension wealth declines, creating spikes in probability of retirement at the early or full retirement ages under the plan. However, it is not straightforward to compare the magnitude of the response across studies. The results regarding the importance of pension wealth on retirement timing are mixed.

Costrell and McGee (2010) apply a reduced-form regression framework to longitudinal administrative data on teachers in Arkansas to estimate the probability of retirement or separation in a given year as a function of pension wealth accrual, pension wealth, and earnings, controlling for age and service. They include two forward-looking pension wealth accrual measures, the one-year accrual rate and the "peak value," a measure of the financial option value of continued work intro-

---

[1]   Another strand of literature finds that teachers' retirement timing is responsive to temporary early retirement incentives, e.g., Furgeson, Strauss, and Vogt, 2006.

duced by Coile and Gruber (2007).[2] In their estimates, a $10,000 present value increase in the peak value (five-year horizon) is associated with a 1–percentage point decrease in the probability of retirement, and a $10,000 increase in the one-year accrual rate is associated with a 0.6–percentage point reduction in retirements. However, the negative association between earnings and retirement dwarfs these effects, and the effect of pension wealth is an order of magnitude smaller and wrong-signed. The model predicts a sharp increase in teacher exits when pension wealth peaks.

Brown (2013a) examines the response of California teachers to a permanent reform of their retirement benefits. Using administrative data, the reduced-form analysis leverages the nonlinearities in benefit accrual and a pension reform–induced shift in the age and service locations of these nonlinearities to identify the impact of the pension on teachers' retirement timing. The results imply that despite the fact that retirements sharply increase around the full-benefits retirement age, teachers' retirement timing is not very sensitive to changes in pension wealth accrual in the short to medium run. The use of a reform in this analysis allows the effect of the pension financial incentives to be decoupled from other features of the pension program and any other factors that are aligned with the pension incentives and independently affect teacher retirement.

The interpretation of the reduced-form and quasi-experimental studies implicitly assumes that individuals are forward-looking and are knowledgeable about their retirement benefits, assumptions maintained in the DRM. However, these studies focus on the timing of retirement and are not well suited to predicting the effect of the defined benefit retirement program on teacher retention over the full career. Specifically, they restrict their sample to near-retirement teachers, and they do not control for selection into the sample based on unobserved differences in preferences (or "taste") for teaching over other alternatives. The responsiveness of novice teachers compared to experienced teachers who are self-selected stayers to pension wealth accrual may

---

[2] The peak value is the maximum possible gain in expected present value of pension wealth that a teacher could earn if he or she continues working.

differ, but these approaches do not allow for this heterogeneity or include the sample in their estimation. The structure of the DRM, on the other hand, allows for taste for teaching to vary across teachers and is estimated on a population of teachers of all experience levels. The estimated model can support policy simulations showing retirement and retention behavior in response to these incentives.

Ni and Podgursky (2015) also estimate a structural model of teacher retirement, making their study the most closely related to ours. They used administrative data that followed nearly 17,000 Missouri teachers aged 47 to 58 for six years to estimate the "option value" model of Stock and Wise (1990). The model assumes a constant relative risk aversion utility function, and utility in a period is a function of the teacher's income (after contribution to retirement) multiplied by a parameter that captures the disutility of working, plus an error term reflecting shocks to income. The disutility-of-working parameter is allowed to change with age, and the model estimates imply that disutility increases approximately linearly with age over the age range of the sample. The authors explain that the disutility-of-work term improves the model fit; Stock and Wise used a similar term in their work for the same reason. A teacher in period t considers when to retire and selects the period, typically a future period, that maximizes the expected value of the present discounted value of utility over the remainder of life. In the form estimated, the error is autoregressive with a one-period lag, which allows for the persistence of factors in the errors such as taste for teaching, health status, or family circumstances. The model was estimated for male and female teachers separately and for the pooled sample. The gender-specific estimates are similar to the pooled estimates. In the pooled-sample estimates, the personal discount rate estimate was 3.5 percent. The disutility of work increases with age; at age 55 one dollar of salary gives the same utility as 70 cents in the retirement benefit, and at age 65 this is 59 cents. For males, the disutility of teaching increases even faster. The value of utility at age 55 is about half the size of the shock standard deviation. The estimated model fits the data well, and Ni and Podgursky use it to simulate the effect of alternative retirement policies such as a shift to a defined contribution retirement benefit.

As the authors recognize, the Stock-Wise model has limitations. First, unlike the DRM, the determination of the optimal period to retire does not allow the individual to reoptimize in future periods depending on the error realizations in those periods. In the DRM, individuals reoptimize in each period, taking account of their current state (age, years of experience, and preference for teaching), teaching and nonteaching pay, the realization of shocks in teaching and non-teaching, and the discounted expected value of preferred choice (maximum) of either continuing in teaching for another period or leaving teaching for a nonteaching job, given possible shock realizations in future periods. Second, like the reduced-form and quasi-experimental approaches, the model does not control for selection into the sample or during the six years over which the sample is followed. In a sample of teachers with nearly 20 years of experience on average, the average preference for teaching is doubtless higher than for a cohort at first entry into teaching. The structure of the DRM allows us to capture this selective retention. Although teachers' taste for teaching in the CPS or random shock terms are not observed, we assume they are distributed according to certain types of probability distributions, and we estimate the distributions' parameters with data on teacher retention over a career. Specifically, we assume tastes for teaching in cohorts of new entrants into CPS are normally distributed, and the random shocks have an extreme-value type 1 distribution. With these distributional assumptions, we can derive expressions for the probability of staying in teaching or, alternatively, leaving teaching, at each year and use these to obtain an expression for the probability of a teaching career with n years of service before leaving. We use these career retention probabilities to construct a likelihood function for estimating the model parameters.

The studies described above estimate the effect of teachers' retirement benefits on retention directly. A related study, Fitzpatrick (2015), estimated teachers' willingness to pay for additional retirement benefits, which is proportional to the influence these benefits have on retirement and other exit decisions. Following the Illinois pension reform in 1998 that increased the generosity of the benefits (the same as that described for Chicago teachers in Appendix A), Illinois teachers had the opportunity to pay a fee to "upgrade" service accrued before the reform to the more generous new benefit schedule. Overall, for teachers with high years of service—the sample Fitzpatrick focuses on— between 70 and 78 percent of near-retirement eligible teachers purchased the upgrade, but the price of the upgrade varied across teachers. Fitzpatrick uses an instrumental variable strategy to estimate the marginal value a teacher placed on the retirement benefit. She finds that teachers were willing to pay 19 cents for an additional, present-value dollar of retirement benefits. Because a present-value dollar of benefits costs a dollar to provide, the results imply that it is highly cost-ineffective to provide more pension benefits on the margin to these teachers in comparison to increasing current compensation. Further, the results imply that these teachers would accept a "buyout" of a portion of pension benefits that would reduce the pension system liabilities. By the same token, teachers would be more responsive to changes in current salary than to changes in retirement benefits.

Teacher Pay and Retention

While defined benefit retirement plans create some of the sharpest financial incentives related to the timing of teacher attrition, especially around retirement age, current salary is an important factor to consider in retention decisions. Teacher retention in a school district is affected by teachers exiting to teach in another school district and teachers leaving teaching altogether, so a teacher's decision will be affected by current teaching salary and the salaries of other teaching and nonteaching employment opportunities. Past estimates of the effect of teacher pay on retention are mixed and seem to depend on the type of retention examined. However, these studies often focus on salary, excluding other (potentially correlated) forms of compensation, like retirement benefits, and they do not employ dynamic programming models but, nevertheless, may be relevant for comparing estimates from the DRM.

Hanushek, Kain, and Rivkin (2004) used student/teacher panel data on Texas public elementary schools, allowing them to control for student demographic and school characteristics and permitting before-

and after-move comparisons for teachers who switch public schools within Texas. With respect to our work, the most relevant salary effect estimates come from a model with controls for district fixed effects and student race/ethnic composition. The salary effects are statistically insignificant except for male teachers with three to five years of experience. These salary effects are relative to the probability of changing districts *or* leaving the Texas public school system entirely, as in our model where the decision is to stay in the Chicago public school system or leave it for another district or a nonteaching job.[3] However, they do find that a higher base-year salary in a district decreases the teacher's probability of leaving for another district, though this tapers with experience.

Hendricks (2015) also uses a panel of teachers in Texas public schools and infers district salary schedules from administrative data. He considers the effect of starting pay (given teacher years of experience) on teacher hiring and turnover; starting pay is higher for a teacher with more years of experience. Using a specification that includes year, district, experience, district-by-year, experience-by-year, and experience-by-district fixed effects, he finds that a 1-percent increase in starting salary has the largest effect on hiring rates of teachers with two to three years of experience, and the effect diminishes as experience increases and becomes insignificant for teachers with nine to 11, 12 to 15, and 16 to 19 years of experience. There is no effect on teachers with zero to one years of experience; Hendricks infers that either these teachers are unresponsive to starting salary, or principals prefer to hire experienced candidates.

Murnane and Olsen (1990) analyze longitudinal data on 13,890 white teachers who began their teaching careers in North Carolina public schools during 1975–1984. They estimate the effect of salary and opportunity cost on teacher retention in the state, where retention is the

---

[3] Hanushek, Kain, and Rivkin view their salary effect estimates with caution. They suggest that the statistical insignificance of the salary effects comes from "an inability to identify the true salary effects from year-to-year salary changes. It is quite plausible that the small year-to-year salary variations provide a noisy measure of the longer-term salary shifts that would affect decisions to quit or change schools, particularly because base year salary is a noisy representation of the entire salary structure" (p. 345).

observed duration in the state's public schools until first absence from any North Carolina school districts; moves between North Carolina districts do not end a teaching spell. Their econometric method allows for right-censored (spells that continue beyond the data window), time-varying covariates (e.g., increases in teachers' salaries), and district-level fixed effects. They proxy opportunity cost using information on the teacher's subject field or National Teachers Exam (NTE) score, assuming the opportunity wage increases with the NTE score—and recognizing that the teacher salary schedule does not depend on NTE score or differ by subject area but does differ across districts.

They find that teachers with higher NTE scores have lower retention, and teachers with higher salaries have higher retention. Specifically, a $1,000 increase in each step of the salary schedule (that is, an across-the-board increase of $1,000 in each step, in 1987 dollars, approximately a 5.6 percent increase), was associated with a two- to three-year increase in median length of stay for a teacher starting in 1975. There is evidence that this effect is weakened when there are fewer opportunities to move between schools and districts, and for teachers with higher NTE scores. Finally, the impact of salary is less when district fixed effects are removed from the model. This suggests that salary differences between schools are in part a compensating differential, where schools with less attractive features tend to pay higher salaries. District fixed effects control for these unobserved differences. Also, there is some interaction between salary and test score: Although higher salary increases retention, this effect is somewhat weaker for teachers with NTE scores in the top quartile.

Stinebrickner (1998) takes the broadest view of retention and employs data from the National Longitudinal Sample of the Class of 1972 (NLS72) and subsequent waves to estimate hazard models of teacher retention in the occupation. The estimation sample comprised 341 individuals who, by 1986, had been certified to teach, and who provided a teaching work history. About 50 percent of the sample had teaching spells lasting more than four years. A one–standard deviation increase in weekly wage increased the probability of staying in teaching more than five years by 9 percent. The average weekly wage was $162, and a one–standard-deviation higher wage was $228, or 40 percent higher.

Related, Chingos and West (2012) analyze the earnings of Florida public school teachers who leave the classroom and find that these leavers earn no more in their new positions. They find that the majority of these teachers continue to be employed by public school districts. However, compared with teaching earnings, the median earnings of those no longer teaching are $9,584 lower for K–8 teachers and $5,827 lower for 9–12 teachers. However, there is significant heterogeneity. The decrease in earnings is much greater for females, and teachers with higher value-added measures earn more after leaving. Further, these estimates are unconditional; that is, they do not control for whether the teacher works full time or part time. The percentage of all exiting teachers for whom earnings data are available is 74 percent—in other words, it seems that about a quarter of leavers do not work. The results from a weighted regression, where the weights are the estimated probability of working full time, show much less earnings change but do not erase the losses: A decrease of $2,291 for K–8 and a gain of $267 for 9–12 for males and females pooled, and decreases of $3,118 for K–8 and $460 for 9–12 for females alone.

For many leavers, the utility of less/no work and lower/no earnings exceeds the utility of teaching as well as the utility of full-time work as a nonteacher. This may be a matter of personal preference, but it also seems likely that external opportunities differ among teachers depending on their field and ability and on the transferability of their teaching human capital. The external wage of many leavers may be low, which is consistent with the idea that teacher training and skills are not general human capital that may be transferred into any other job. In this case, a leaver, faced with a choice set of low-wage jobs, may choose to work part time or not at all.

Teacher Retention and School Attributes

Several studies provide evidence that school characteristics, particularly those linked to working conditions, affect teacher retention. Hanushek,

Kain, and Rivkin (2004) find that teacher movement between schools or exit from teaching is far more strongly related to student characteristics, especially race and achievement, than to salary. In their Texas public school data, salaries increase on average by (only) 0.5 percent when a teacher moves from one district to another, whereas there is a larger percentage change in measures related to race and achievement: "...teachers systematically favor higher achieving, nonminority, non low-income students" (p. 337). For the average mover from one district to another, district average achievement is about 0.07 standard deviations higher in the destination district than in the origin district, which is 3 percentile points higher on the state distribution. Teachers in a school at the bottom achievement quartile are more likely to leave than those in the top quartile—almost 20 percent of teachers in the bottom-quartile schools leave each year compared with slightly more than 15 percent in the top-quartile schools—and much of this reflects transfers to another school in the same district.

This finding may have implications for our analysis. Chicago is a large school district, and teachers can transfer between schools depending on openings. Longer-serving teachers in Chicago public schools may have transferred from one school to another one or more times during their teaching career. Because transfers occur over a career, retention and movement up the salary schedule may be correlated with utility-increasing moves, and not controlling for student achievement, or, more broadly, school fixed effects, might cause an upward bias in our estimates of teachers' mean taste for teaching in Chicago.

Loeb, Darling-Hammond, and Luczak (2005) have a complementary finding based on California teacher survey data linked to district data on salaries and staffing patterns and demographic factors. Their objective is to use the survey data to parse out the influence of salary and working conditions apart from school-level student characteristics (e.g., achievement, proportion of low-income students, racial composition). The study finds that lower salaries and working conditions including large class size, facilities problems, multitrack schools, and lack of textbooks predict higher teacher turnover. Accounting for these conditions decreases the influence of student characteristics. However, the study does not use actual measures of teacher turnover but employs survey responses on whether teachers report their school has a serious problem with teacher turnover, that vacancies are hard to fill, and on the proportion of beginning teachers in the school.

Schools have also introduced induction and mentoring programs that provide starting teachers with support and orientation to help them learn about their new local environment, with the objective of improving their classroom teaching practices and increasing their retention. The use of induction and mentoring grew rapidly in the 1990s. Two-fifths of new teachers received induction assistance in 1990, and nearly four-fifths received it in 2000 (Smith and Ingersoll, 2004). In turn, this should improve their effectiveness as teachers, resulting in higher student achievement, and decrease the turnover-related turbulence faced by students, because their teachers are less likely to leave. Ingersoll and Strong (2011) critically reviewed the research on these programs. They screened the literature and selected 15 empirical studies. Many of the nonselected studies were based only on outcomes from participants in the programs, while those included in the study had outcome data from both participants and nonparticipants. Most of these studies found a positive impact of induction and mentoring on teacher retention, instructional practices, and student achievement. However, a large randomized controlled trial (RCT) of induction in a sample of large, urban, low-income schools found no effect on retention or classroom practices, despite some positive effects on student achievement. The authors suggest that because the control group in the RCT followed the usual practices of induction, which might have been similar to the induction treatment, the treatment might have had little effect relative to the control.

One of the studies reviewed by Ingersoll and Strong concerned induction programs in Chicago Public Schools, by Kapadia, Coca, and Easton (2007). Even though all teachers were supposed to receive induction, 20 percent reported that they were not in a formal induction program. Regression estimates showed no statistically significant difference in outcomes between those reporting none versus those reporting induction, after controlling for teacher, classroom, and school factors. The outcomes were self-reported and included how positive a teacher's first year on the job was, and the teacher's intentions to stay in teaching and stay in the same school. The level of induction and mentoring was divided into three groups—weak, average, and strong—and of teachers receiving induction, those receiving strong induction had better outcomes on all three measures.

Further, the Kapadia, Coca, and Easton study found that novice teachers were assigned more demanding classrooms than nonnovice teachers. A higher percentage of students were below norms in reading and in math, and the median reading and math percentiles were lower. For instance, the percentage of students in class below norms in reading was 71 percent for novice teachers and 62 percent for nonnovice teachers, and the median reading percentile of the class was 36 for novice teachers and 41 for nonnovice teachers.

Teacher Retention by Teacher Effectiveness

Ronfeldt, Loeb, and Wyckoff (2013) find that teacher turnover has a negative effect on student achievement, and this is not confined to classrooms where the teacher left but extends to students whose teachers have remained in the school. These adverse effects are more pronounced in schools with higher proportions of low-performing and African-American students. The estimates suggest that the teachers' prior effectiveness explains some of this effect, i.e., relatively more high-performing teachers were likely to leave the schools with higher proportions of low-performing and African-American students.

However, Boyd et al. (2011); Feng and Sass (2012); Goldhaber, Gross, and Player (2011); and Hanushek, Kain, and Rivkin (2004) find that teachers more effective in teaching their students are more likely to stay. Goldhaber, Gross, and Player, for instance, find that teachers with higher value added are more likely to stay at their initial school and to remain in the teaching profession, but there is heterogeneity in teacher mobility across the value-added distribution. Papay et al. (2015) find that more-effective teachers are more likely to remain in their districts and their schools. Their measure of teacher effectiveness comes from a value-added model producing an empirical Bayes estimate of a teacher's effectiveness based on the first two years of teaching. The results vary across districts, as was the case with retention in general. But Steele et al. (2015) find teacher outflow from schools to be neutral with respect to the teacher's value added—schools with higher turnover are not disproportionately losing their best teachers. Even so, Steele et al. (2015) also report disparities across schools within a district with respect to teachers' qualifications and value added.[4]

Koedel, Podgursky, and Shi (2013) examine the link between teachers' pension incentives and workforce quality in Missouri. They test whether the structure of the retirement benefits incentivizes highly effective teachers to prolong their careers and/or encourages teachers who are less effective to exit. Using student-level panel data from Missouri, this study finds no evidence that teachers who seem to be "retained" by the pension financial incentives improve student achievement more (as measured by value added) than teachers who appear to be "pushed out" of teaching by the pension financial incentives. However, the sample size and specification used in the analysis results in a test for identifying effectiveness that has low statistical power, so large differences in effectiveness are not ruled out. Also, there is no clear counterfactual, which makes it difficult to know whether the pension is better at retaining effective teachers or maintaining an effective workforce than an alternative retirement system. Finally, although this paper controls for students' previous achievement, retirement may be endogenous to student performance or to other factors that affect student performance.

Fitzpatrick and Lovenheim (2014) and Brown (2013b) both examine the effect of retirements induced by pension reforms on student achievement. Fitzpatrick and Lovenheim examine the effect of a temporary retirement incentive in Illinois in the mid-1990s. This

---

[4] "Compared to a student whose school is in the lowest quartile of minority enrollment, a student who attends a school in the highest quartile has access to teachers with about three years less experience, about a 10 percentage-point higher chance of being a novice, about a 10 percentage-point lower chance of having an advanced degree, and about a 6 percentage-point lower chance of having attended a competitive college. Perhaps more importantly, the student has access to teachers whose value-added is about 11% of a student-level standard deviation lower than those of his peers in the lowest minority enrollment quartile. These are meaningful differences that seem likely to exacerbate racial/ethnic achievement gaps" (p. 99).

incentive allowed teachers to purchase an extra five years of age and experience to be counted as creditable service for calculating their retirement benefit, conditional on immediate retirement. This incentive was most generous for highly experienced teachers, and approximately 10 percent of teachers left Illinois public school systems in the two-year time span during which the incentive was in place. Based on this relationship between teaching experience and take-up of the early retirement incentive, the authors define treatment at the school-grade level as the number of teachers with more than 15 years of experience in that school-grade (as measured preincentive) and use a difference-in-differences estimation approach. The results indicate that there was no reduction in the test scores of students entering school-grades that had more incentive-induced retirements.

Brown (2013b) uses a similar approach and examines the effect of retirements on student achievement in California. An unexpected pension reform in the late 1990s permanently increased the retirement benefits of teachers over age 60 and with 30 or more years of service by as much as 20 percent overnight, providing an incentive for this set of highly experienced teachers to retire earlier than planned. The instrumental variable results imply that pension-induced teacher retirements had a positive effect on student achievement. Together these findings suggest that the retirement timing of less effective teachers is more responsive to unexpected increases in pension benefits.

Mansfield (2015) uses administrative data from North Carolina public high schools to analyze whether the allocation of teachers within and across the schools affects student test scores. He finds that teaching quality is "fairly equitably distributed" in the sense that average teacher quality explains a small fraction of performance gaps across schools. Mansfield suggests several reasons the distribution of teacher quality is not greatly different across schools: Teachers within a district all face the same salary schedule; teachers and schools might have inadequate information about teacher quality/school quality at the time of hiring, and it is difficult for administrators to fire underperforming teachers; teachers may have diverse preferences regarding what they like in a school; and teachers are hired by districts, not schools, and transfers between schools may reflect the preferences of administrators more than those of teachers. But within a school, the variation in teacher quality does affect test score variance. A student with a teacher who is one standard deviation above average (measured by value added) can expect a higher test score, enough for the average student to move from the 50th to the 57th percentile of the state test score distribution. Still, over the course of high school, a student will have teachers above and below average quality, on net causing only a small difference in the student's overall test score performance.

Conclusion

The literature on teachers is vast, and indeed there are journals devoted to education research as well as to the economics of education, education finance, human resources, and more. The articles we have discussed are an introduction to the literature, and although our review is by no means comprehensive, it touches on many key issues and findings related to our analysis. Perhaps the broadest insight from the literature with respect to this paper lies in the absence of any article applying a dynamic programming framework to teacher retention. The closest work is the structural model of Ni and Podgursky, and we are in full agreement with their observation that the structural literature on pensions and the timing of retirement has not extended to teachers. Further, the literature on teacher retention focuses primarily on factors related to turnover, e.g., school and student characteristics, teacher qualification and productivity, and current pay. As important as these factors are, the models are not well suited to support counterfactual policy analysis to predict the effect on teacher retention of changes in the retirement benefit system or the level and structure of current compensation, or to calculate the cost of such changes. We therefore conclude that the DRM, with its capability to model teacher retention over an entire career and support simulations showing the retention effects and cost of counterfactual policies, can be a useful addition to the literature.

CHAPTER FOUR
A Dynamic Retention Model of Chicago Public School Teacher Retention

The dynamic programming approach has been used in recent years in economics and management,[1] and more extensively in defense manpower to analyze retention of active- and reserve-component military personnel and Department of Defense civil service employees.[2,3,4] To the best of our knowledge, it has not been used to analyze and assess compensation policies for public school teachers.[5] This chapter describes a DRM of CPS teachers. It begins with the theoretical DRM for teachers. The estimation methodology is then described. Model estimates and fit are presented in Chapter Six, while Chapter Five discusses the sample and teacher and nonteacher wage profiles.

---

[1] See, for example, Hotz and Miller, 1993; Rust, 1994; Keane and Wolpin, 1997; Aguirregabiria and Mira, 2010; Bajari, Benkard, and Levin, 2007; Van der Klaauw, 2012; and Borkovsky, Doraszelski, and Kryukov, 2012.

[2] See, for example, Asch, Mattock, and Hosek, 2013; Asch et al., 2008; Mattock, Hosek, and Asch, 2012; Mattock and Arkes, 2007; and Gotz and McCall, 1984.

[3] The first recorded application of this methodology was a study of U.S. Air Force officer retention in Gotz and McCall, 1984, as acknowledged in Rust, 1994.

[4] See Asch, Mattock, and Hosek, 2014a.

[5] As mentioned in Chapter Three, Ni and Podgursky (2015) used a Stock-Wise–style model. Although this model selects an optimal exit date as of the information available in the initial period (age) at which the individual is observed, it does not permit reoptimization in each future period and therefore differs from a stochastic dynamic programming model such as the one we use.

A Dynamic Retention Model of Chicago Public School Teacher Retention

The DRM is an econometric model of retention behavior. In it, employees make retention decisions each year over their career with a given employer. The model assumes that these employees are rational and forward-looking, taking into account their expected future earnings from the employer, as well as their own preference for employment with that employer, and uncertainty about future events that could cause them to value their current service more or less, relative to their external opportunities. Once the parameters of the underlying decision process, described later, are estimated, we can use these estimates to simulate the baseline retention profile of an entry cohort of CPS teachers, as well as the retention profile under alternative compensation policies, such as changes to the retirement system. By appropriately scaling the results, we can make inferences about the effect of those policies on the size of the workforce retained and the required number of additional hires needed to sustain the workforce should it decrease. While we do not explicitly model hiring, the effect of the policy on the required number of hires is completely determined by the change in retention.

A basic version of the DRM used in the military context is the foundation of the DRM we develop for teachers. This basic version has been described in a number of past studies (see, for example, Mattock and Arkes, 2007) but has not been described in the context of the public school teachers, so we explain it in some detail here for readers unfamiliar with those other studies. The discussion gives a broad overview, followed by the technical details of the model. The basic version models teacher retention from the start of employees' careers as teachers in CPS, or "new entrants." While we did not model the decision whether to or when to enter CPS as a teacher, employees in the model can become CPS teachers for the first time at any age. But in the estimation we focus on the subset of teachers in our data who entered CPS between the ages of 22 and 30. These teachers are largely at the outset of their career as a teacher, whereas teachers who enter CPS at a later age might have begun teaching earlier in a different school district or perhaps decided to become a teacher after having experience in a different occupational path. The teachers who enter at a later age might therefore be a differently selected population.

We extended this basic model so that it is suitable for a mixed sample of teachers that consists of new-entrant teachers as well as incumbent teachers at a point in time. The included incumbent teachers are the subset of teachers who were new entrants when they entered CPS as teachers in an earlier year and were between the ages of 22 and 30 at entry. The advantage of the mixed sample is that a significant fraction of the incumbent teachers reach the retirement window in the period covered by the data. In contrast, the vast majority of teachers in the new-entrant sample do not reach the retirement window in the period covered by the data—they are not followed long enough—hence, their retirement behavior cannot be observed.

Each year, the individual compares the value of continuing to be a CPS teacher with that of leaving and bases his or her decision on which alternative has the maximum value. In the basic DRM, we model teacher retention up to the teacher's first departure from teaching in CPS.[6] Individuals who stay can revisit the choice between teaching in CPS and external opportunities in each future period until either retirement from the labor force, which is presumed to be at age 66, or retirement from CPS, which for many teachers is at 34 years of service when retirement benefits attain their maximum value. All of these decisions will depend on the employee's unique circumstances at a given point in time. Those circumstances include an individual's preference for teaching in CPS relative to external opportunities and random events that may affect relative preference.

In the model, the value of staying depends on the annual teacher earnings in each time period. Annual earnings depend on years of service in CPS. A teacher who began her career at an older age would have the same pay as her younger counterparts with the same cumulative

---

[6] However, some teachers who leave might reenter at a later date. The DRM structure can be adapted to handle this, and it is a possible topic for future research. Also, teachers may take authorized leave from CPS. If the observed time away from CPS was two years or less before the teacher again appears in the data, we assumed the leave was authorized.

years of service. The value of staying also depends on the individual's preference for teaching in CPS relative to the external market (his or her "taste" for teaching in CPS) and a period- and individual-specific environmental disturbance term (or shock) that can either positively or negatively affect the value placed on teaching in that period. For example, having an ailing family member who requires assistance with home care could be such a shock. The taste for teaching is assumed to be constant over time for a given individual and can be thought of as the net effect of idiosyncratic, persistent differences related to the individual's perceived value of working in CPS relative to the external market. The net effect includes all nonmonetary and monetary factors the individual perceives as relevant to teaching in CPS over and above monetary factors included in the model. These factors might include an interest in reaching children during their formative years, positive and negative aspects the individual perceives about teaching in CPS (e.g., hours of work, paid leave, an annual schedule centered on the academic calendar), and persistent differences in CPS teacher and private-sector earnings apart from the differences accounted for in the model. As mentioned, we use a single curve to represent teacher salary and external salary by age. But an individual might believe his or her teacher and external salaries are persistently higher or lower than those curves. The net effect of these perceived differences would enter into taste. Another way of describing taste, then, is as a person-specific fixed effect.

The model assumes that the teacher's mandatory 2-percent contribution from her salary (discussed in Chapter Two) to her CTPF pension shifts her permanent taste for teaching. Alternatively, it could have been modeled as a reduction to the teacher's salary of 2 percent. Since the contribution is mandatory for all teachers, whether the pension is applied to the salary directly or indirectly through a shift in the taste distribution, the effect on the probability of a teacher staying in CPS is similar.[7]

---

[7]   The shift in taste is a level shift, whereas the CTPF contribution is a percentage of teacher pay. We expect the effect of this misspecification to be small, because teacher contributions range from $906 in year of service 1 to $1,772 in year of service 30, which are small relative to the mean taste, which is estimated to be greater than $26,000 (see Figure 6.2).

Individuals are heterogeneous with respect to their tastes for teaching in CPS, i.e., their tastes differ. As we discuss below, we as analysts do not directly observe these tastes, but we assume they are distributed according to a known type of probability distribution but with unknown parameters. A goal of the estimation process is to estimate these parameters.

The value of staying as a CPS teacher also includes the value of the option to leave at a later date. That is, the individual knows that he or she can revisit and reoptimize the decision to stay or leave in each future period. Of course, the future is uncertain, so the value of being able to choose to stay or leave in the future is expressed as the discounted present value of an expected value. Individuals may reoptimize, and might change their decision in the future because new information, e.g., a new shock, makes it reasonable to do so or because the discounted expected value of future benefits of leaving becomes greater relative to the benefits of staying.

There is also a shock related to the external opportunity. Thus, there are two sources of uncertainty to the individual teacher. These are the shock to the value of staying in teaching and the shock to the value of leaving teaching. Shocks are drawn each period. Shocks in past periods and in the current period have been realized—the individual knows their values. Future shocks are realized only in future periods, but the individual is assumed to know the shock distributions and uses this information to form a rational guess about the option value of staying, namely, the expected value of the maximum from being able to reoptimize (choose the better alternative) in each future period. The expected value is not uncertain; it is an expected value calculation made by the individual given knowledge of the shock distributions.

Importantly, choices made today can affect the value of choices in the future. A teacher who chooses to stay in CPS today adds a year of service, moving closer to retirement eligibility and increasing retirement benefits, thereby influencing the value of choosing teaching in CPS in the future. Similarly, past choices can affect the value of current and future choices.

The value of leaving includes the value of the external alternative, which includes pay in the external market (or the forgone value of pay if the individual decides not to stay in the labor market), any CPS retirement benefits the individual is entitled to receive, and an individual- and period-specific shock term that can either positively or negatively affect preference for the external alternative.[8] Pay in the external market varies with age, with those entering CPS at older ages having higher external pay opportunities. Entry age can also affect how soon CPS retirement benefits are available to an entering individual.

An individual who leaves CPS might remain in teaching, obtain work in a different occupation, work full or part time, or leave the labor force. In the current analysis, we use the earnings of full-time nonteachers in the Chicago metropolitan area to represent external earnings.

More formally, we can write the value of staying a CPS teacher for an individual of age a at time t as

$$V_{a,t}^{S} = \gamma^{c} + w_{t}^{c} + \beta E_{t}\left[Max\left(V_{a+1,t+1}^{S}, V_{a+1,t+1}^{L}\right)\right] + \varepsilon_{t}^{c}, \qquad (4.1)$$

where

$V_{a,t}^{S}$ is the value of staying a teacher in CPS at age a and time t,

γ^{c} is individual taste for CPS teaching relative to the external market,

w_{t}^{c} is CPS teacher annual earnings at time t (and experience in CPS is also t),

β is the teacher's personal discount factor,

$V_{a+1,t+1}^{S}$ is the value of staying as a teacher in CPS at age $a + 1$ and time $t + 1$,

$V_{a+1,t+1}^{L}$ is the value of leaving teaching in CPS at age $a + 1$ and time $t + 1$,

$E_{t}\left[Max\left(V_{a+1,t+1}^{S}, V_{a+1,t+1}^{L}\right)\right]$ is the expected value of having the option to choose to stay or leave in the next period, and

ε_{t}^{c} is the random shock to CPS teacher employment at time t.

Similarly, the value of leaving teaching in CPS at age a and time t is

---

[8]   We also considered including the potential Social Security benefit, but for reasons we discuss in Chapter Six, we chose to omit it in the final analysis.

$$V_{a,t}^{L} = w_a^e + \Sigma_{s=a+1}^{A}\beta^{s-a}w_s^e + R_{a,t}^c + \varepsilon_t^e, \qquad (4.2)$$

where

$V_{a,t}^{L}$ is the value of leaving CPS teaching at age a and time t,

w_a^e is annual earnings in the external market at age a plus retirement benefits that will accrue to the public school teacher in the external market from a until A,

$\Sigma_{s=a+1}^{A}\beta^{s-a}w_s^e$ is the present value of future external market earnings,

$R_{a,t}^c$ is the retirement benefit accrued as a result of teaching in CPS for an individual leaving at age a and time t with total service as a teacher in CPS t (exclusive of any benefit accrued from work in the external market; if the individual cannot collect CPS retirement benefits due to her age, this is the present value of the retirement benefit),

ε_t^e is the random shock to external employment at time t.

Consistent with policy, equation 4.2 assumes that to claim CPS teacher retirement benefits, the individual must have left CPS.

An individual decides to continue teaching in CPS at age a and time t if the value of staying is greater than the value of leaving, or

stay at age a and time t if $V_{a,t}^{S} = \max\left(V_{a,t}^{S}, V_{a,t}^{L}\right)$.

Thus, the probability of staying a teacher in CPS at age a at time t is

$$\Pr_{a,t}\left(Stay\right) = \Pr\left(V_{a,t}^{S} > V_{a,t}^{L}\right) = \Pr\left(E\left(V_{a,t}^{S}\right) - E\left(V_{a,t}^{L}\right) > \varepsilon_t^e - \varepsilon_t^c\right). \quad (4.3)$$

Referring back to Equations 4.1 and 4.2, we see that the current wage enters the value function linearly and has a coefficient of one. However, the decision to stay depends not only on the current wage but also on the value of the entire value function, which also incorporates taste, current shock, and the expected value of the maximum in the next period. Although the model's structure may seem simple because the current wage enters additively, it is in fact complex, and the stay/leave decision depends on a full assessment of current and future opportunities. As shown later, the model fits teacher retention data well.

More-complex model specifications have been used in other work. For instance, dynamic programming has been applied to analyze retirement decisions and full- versus part-time work choices (van der Klaauw and Wolpin, 2008). Such models use a period-specific utility function, and the objective is to maximize intertemporal utility subject to initial assets, saving behavior, and the retirement system, e.g., Social Security. Such specifications are potentially useful for analyzing teacher retention, but available data limit what can be done. Data on spouse earnings, full- versus part-time work, savings, wealth, and the timing of retirement are absent, for example. Stated differently, our value-function specification can be thought of as a particular form of utility function in which current utility depends additively on the current wage, taste, and shock, plus the discounted expected value of following the best path in the next period.

We do not observe individuals' tastes for teaching in CPS or random shock terms. Instead, we assume they are each distributed according to known types of probability distributions with unknown parameters that we estimate using available data. Specifically, we assume individuals' tastes for teaching in CPS are normally distributed and the random shocks have an extreme-value type 1 distribution. Given these distributional assumptions, we can derive choice probabilities for each alternative at each decision year and the cumulative choice probabilities or survival probabilities for an entering cohort at each decision year and then write an appropriate likelihood equation to estimate the parameters of the model. These include the standard deviation of the probability distribution for the shock terms, the mean and standard deviation for the distribution of taste for teaching in CPS for new-entrant teachers at entry, and the discount factor.

We next present the choice probabilities, the cumulative retention probabilities, and the likelihood equation. The extreme-value distribution, $EV[a,b]$, has the form $\exp(-\exp((a-x/b))$ with a mean of $a+b\Gamma$ and a variance of $\pi^2 b^2/6$ (or a standard deviation of $\frac{\pi b}{\sqrt{6}} \approx 1.28b$), where Γ is Euler's Gamma (approximately 0.577), a is the location parameter, and b is the scale parameter. We assume the shock terms have a zero mean and scale λ, implying that they have the extreme-value distribution $EV[-\Gamma\lambda,\lambda]$, i.e., $a=-\Gamma\lambda$ and $b=\lambda$. Since both ε_t^e and ε_t^c have an extreme-value distribution, the difference $\varepsilon_t^e - \varepsilon_t^c$ in Equation 4.3 is known to have a logistic distribution. With this information, the expected value of the maximum of $V_{a+1,t+1}^S$ and $V_{a+1,t+1}^L$ can be written as

$$E_t\left[Max\left(V_{a+1,t+1}^S, V_{a+1,t+1}^L\right)\right] = \iint Max\left(V_{a+1,t+1}^S, V_{a+1,t+1}^L\right) d\varepsilon_t^c d\varepsilon_t^e$$

$$= \lambda \ln\left[e^{\frac{V_{a+1,t+1}^S}{\lambda}} + e^{\frac{V_{a+1,t+1}^L}{\lambda}}\right]. \quad (4.4)$$

Consequently, we can write the expected value of $V_{a,t}^S$ as

$$E\left[V_{a,t}^S\right] = \gamma^c + w_t^c + \beta\lambda \ln\left[e^{\frac{V_{a+1,t+1}^S}{\lambda}} + e^{\frac{V_{a+1,t+1}^L}{\lambda}}\right]. \quad (4.5)$$

Thus, we have an explicit expression for the value function, given (unobserved to the analyst) taste for teaching in CPS, γ^c. (Later in this chapter, we describe how we handle unobserved tastes by integrating out this source of heterogeneity.) Given Equation 4.5, we can write the probability that a teacher chooses to stay at age a and time t as

$$\Pr_{a,t}(Stay) = \frac{e^{\frac{V_{a,t}^S}{\lambda}}}{e^{\frac{V_{a,t}^S}{\lambda}} + e^{\frac{V_{a,t}^L}{\lambda}}}. \quad (4.6)$$

The probability of leaving at age a and time t is $1 - \Pr_{a,t}(Stay)$.

Given these probabilities, we can write the cumulative probability that a CPS teacher entering at time 1 with age a will stay through t as

$$cumulative\,\Pr(Stay)_{a,t} = \Pi_{s=1}^t \Pr_{a+s-1,s}(Stay). \quad (4.7)$$

The cumulative probability that a CPS teacher who enters at age a stays for $t-1$ years and leaves at t is

$$cumulative \, \Pr(Leave)_{a,t} = \Pi_{s=1}^{t-1} \Pr_{a+s-1,s}\left(Stay\right)\left(1 - \Pr_{a+t-1,t}\left(Stay\right)\right).$$

(4.8)

These probabilities are conditioned on the unobserved taste parameter, γ^c, since the value of staying, V_t^S, depends on γ^c. As mentioned, we assume the taste parameter has a normal distribution $g(\gamma^c)$ with mean μ and standard deviation σ. We use this information to formulate the expected cumulative probability of a given career path, or the likelihood of that path. Thus, for a teacher in our data who enters teaching at age a, stays through $t - 1$, and leaves at t, the likelihood of that career path is

$$\mathcal{L}_i\left(\mu,\sigma,\lambda,\beta\right) = \int_{-\infty}^{\infty} \Pi_{s=1}^{t-1} \Pr_{a+s-1,s}\left(Stay\right)\left(1 - \Pr_{a+t-1,t}\left(Stay\right)\right)g\left(\gamma^c\right)d\gamma^c.$$

(4.9)

The subscript i in $\mathcal{L}_i$ denotes the ith teacher in our data. Similarly, if the individual stays through t and is then censored, the likelihood is

$$\mathcal{L}_i\left(\mu,\sigma,\lambda,\beta\right) = \int_{-\infty}^{\infty} \Pi_{s=1}^{t} \Pr_{a+s-1,s}\left(Stay\right)g\left(\gamma^c\right)d\gamma^c.$$

(4.10)

Thus, the likelihood for the entire data sample, N, is given by

$$\mathcal{L}\left(\mu,\sigma,\lambda,\beta\right) = \Pi_{i=1}^{N}\mathcal{L}_i\left(\mu,\sigma,\lambda,\beta\right).$$

(4.11)

The discussion so far has been relevant to a population observed at entry into teaching in CPS and assumes that members of the population are represented by the same taste distribution. Extending the DRM to incumbent teachers recognizes that their taste distribution is conditional on having taught for some years. In our particular extension, we want to add incumbent teachers present in the first year of our sample who joined CPS as a new entrant in an earlier year, and we maintain the assumption that their taste distribution at entry was the same as the taste distribution of current new entrants.[9] Under this assumption, we can express their conditional taste distribution in terms of the new entrant taste distribution and the cumulative probability of individuals with a given taste staying in CPS until the year of service when they are first observed, and this will allow us to incorporate incumbent teachers into our sample and likelihood function.

The density of taste, γ^c, in year of service t conditional on staying continuously from year of service one to $t - 1$ is

$$p(\gamma^c \mid s_1, s_2, \ldots s_{t-1}) = p(\gamma^c, s_1, s_2, \ldots s_{t-1}) / p(s_1, s_2, \ldots s_{t-1})$$
$$= p(s_1, s_2, \ldots s_{t-1} \mid \gamma^c) g(\gamma^c) / p(s_1, s_2, \ldots s_{t-1}).$$

Here, $p(s_1, s_2, \ldots s_{t-1} \mid \gamma^c)$ is the probability that a teacher stays continuously for $t-1$ years of service given a particular value of taste drawn at the start of work as a teacher in CPS, that is, as a new entrant, and the density of taste for new entrants is $g(\gamma^c)$. (We use "s" instead of "*Stay*" for a more compact format.) The denominator, $p(s_1, s_2, \ldots s_{t-1})$, is the probability of staying for $t - 1$ years of service continuously averaged over all values of taste; that is, taste is integrated out.

The DRM is a first-order Markov process; hence the probability of staying in year $t - 1$ given that one has stayed continuously from year one to $t - 2$ is just the probability of staying in $t - 1$ given staying in $t - 2$. The prior history is fully accounted by the teacher's state in $t - 1$, defined by years of service at that time, age, and taste. Let $p(s_{t-1})$ be the probability of staying in $t - 2$; the "$t - 2$" is not shown. With this notation,

$$p(s_1, s_2, \ldots s_{t-1} \mid \gamma^c) g(\gamma^c) = p(s_{t-1} \mid \gamma^c) p(s_{t-2} \mid \gamma^c) \ldots p(s_1 \mid \gamma^c) g(\gamma^c).$$

Moreover, since the particular taste is drawn from the new-entrant taste distribution, a fuller statement of the same expression includes the mean and standard deviation of that distribution:

---

[9]   This is potentially testable for large-enough sample sizes. The test would be whether the taste parameters, namely, the mean and standard deviation of taste, are statistically equal across the entry cohorts. This is beyond the scope of our current work.

$$p\left(s_{t-1} \mid \gamma^c;\mu,\sigma\right)p\left(s_{t-2} \mid \gamma^c;\mu,\sigma\right)...p\left(s_1 \mid \gamma^c;\mu,\sigma\right)g\left(\gamma^c;\mu,\sigma\right)$$

Each of the stay probabilities on the right-hand side has the form shown in Equation 4.6. Thus, for given values of μ and σ, we can compute the stay probabilities and the taste density at γ^c.

Finally, the probability shown can be interpreted as the probability of observing an incumbent teacher as of a given calendar year. For example, consider incumbent teachers in 1992. Again, the incumbent teachers we are interested in are those who were CPS new entrants in an earlier calendar year, were aged 22 to 30 when they entered, and stayed continuously to the current calendar year. A teacher in year of service 20 in 1992 had her first year of service in 1973. The probability of observing this teacher as of 1992 is

$$\int_{-\infty}^{\infty} p\left(s_{19} \mid \gamma^c\right)p\left(s_{18} \mid \gamma^c\right)...p\left(s_1 \mid \gamma^c\right)g\left(\gamma^c\right)d\gamma^c .$$

Probability expressions for retention decisions in years from 1992 forward can be appended to this probability to obtain a full probability expression for the individual's career retention in CPS, and the full expression (divided by a normalizing constant—the cumulative probability of survival over all tastes until year of service 20) can be included in the likelihood function.

Identification

Our discussion of identification begins with a discussion motivating the issue of identification in structural models, then discusses identification in the context of our specific model.

The DRM has features that differentiate it from a one-period, single equation model of the sort used in the studies of teacher turnover that we reviewed. In particular, the DRM assumes an individual objective function and decisionmaking behavior. The objective function involves a teacher selecting the better alternative, teaching or nonteaching, in each period in which the individual is a teacher. The teacher's assessment of the alternatives is forward-looking, time-consistent, accounts for uncertainty, and permits reoptimization in future periods. Further, the empirical implementation of the DRM requires longitudinal data on teachers over their teaching careers, or, more specifically, over their CPS teaching careers. Because the objective function and decisionmaking behavior are assumed, they are not objects to be estimated. Instead, estimation focuses on finding parameters relevant to the population of teachers at entry into CPS. These parameters are identifiable from the retention data and include the entering-teacher population taste distribution, average personal discount rate, variance of shocks, switching cost, and parameters describing the population's initial, transitory taste for teaching (motivation for this additional parameter is described in Chapter Six). The parameters are estimated simultaneously, and the estimated parameters are the ones that fit the data best given the objective function and decisionmaking behavior. With the estimated parameters for the population of teachers at entry and the assumed decisionmaking structure, it is possible to simulate the retention effect of changes to the current teacher compensation and retirement policy, i.e., it is possible to do counterfactual analyses. The estimated parameters are empirically grounded, and the utility of the model can be judged by goodness of fit. This is not to conclude that the specification is uniquely best, though we explored alternative specifications and selected the one that performed best.

The estimation of one-period, single-equation models also involves trying alternative specifications to obtain a good fit. These models typically do not assume an objective function or a decisionmaking behavior such as dynamic programming. The purpose may be to describe the relationship between the explanatory variables and the dependent variable, or to estimate the causal effect of a particular variable using other variables as controls. Propensity-score matched samples and doubly robust models are examples of methods for this, and they require exogenous variation in the variable of interest or an instrument for it, to identify the causal effect.

Causal methods for single-equation models are now in common use. In contrast, structural models are often used when there is no existing empirical variation to support causal inference but when it is satisfactory to assume that the model of decisionmaking can be credibly applied under alternative policies (the incentive structure changes but individuals continue to behave rationally), and the population and shock parameters remain relevant (shifting to a different incentive structure does not alter population tastes, discount rate, shocks, or switching costs).[10]

For the DRM, we estimate the taste distribution (mean and variance of taste) of the entry population of teachers, the variance of the shock distributions, and the average personal discount rate. These parameters are assumed invariant to changes in teacher compensation and personnel policies, permitting the researcher to simulate the retention response to changes in policy. A simulation of retention decisions given a wage increase will reveal the responsiveness of retention to the wage increase while the underlying parameters have not changed. Viewed this way, identification of a structural model relies on the underlying parameters being identified, not the policy response.

With respect to the underlying parameters, the average personal discount rate is the only within-person preference parameter in the DRM that captures the weighting of decisions across time. Variation in entry age means that pension eligibility will occur at different ages and external opportunities will vary by age (i.e., the nonteaching wage). The average personal discount factor reflects the trade-off between a higher nonteaching wage today and greater lifetime pension benefits in the future. Importantly, this parameter captures how an individual values benefits that have payoffs long into the future, such as pensions. If an individual did not value the future, then greater pension benefits would have no value to the individual. No other parameter in the model captures this variation.

The model identifies the mean and variance of teacher taste from the observed differences in retention among individuals after controlling for their current and expected future teacher pay and retirement

---

[10]   Going beyond this observation, structural models can be estimated on data generated by a randomized controlled trial or a quasi-experiment when such data are available. In using such data, the model coding is adapted to each policy, but the underlying population, hence the population parameters, would be assumed to remain the same. As with the analysis of data from RCTs or quasi-experiments, this could require the weighting of samples or propensity score matching to make them comparable.

benefits and nonteacher pay. As mentioned, one could think of the mean and standard deviation of taste as being the analogue of the fixed effect in a random-effects regression model, reflecting person-specific, unobserved heterogeneity. Similarly, the shock variance would be the analogue of the error variance in the random-effects model. In this sense, the taste distribution and shock variance capture what is left unexplained by the structure of the model (preferences, pay and pension incentives, and the dynamic program that allows individuals to reoptimize in each period). Where our model differs from the random-effect model analogue is that the decision process is repeated from entry age until the individual exits teaching, and of course the model covers the teacher's entire work life.

The early-career taste factor is identified from differences in retention among individuals after controlling for permanent taste and teacher and nonteacher incentives. Finally, the shock variance is identified from the variation in retention at each state not explained by pay and tastes (i.e., the intertemporal residual).

The response to a change in compensation policy is determined by the structure of the model. Threats to identification come from model misspecification, which would bias the model's parameter estimates and any policy simulations based on those estimates. If, for example, the earnings profile of a teacher was too high in the later part of a teacher's career, the model might place too little weight on the mean taste for teaching. The impact of a higher pension contribution might then lead to lower retention than what would have been produced with a greater mean taste for teaching. Examining the fit and sensitivity of the policy response to alternative structural assumptions helps to determine the robustness of the parameters and simulated policy effects.

In Chapter Six, we consider alternative model specifications to produce a better fit to the data. In achieving a close fit to observed data, the implication is that the chosen structure in our structural model is sufficient to capture the retention profiles of CPS teachers.

Estimation

The parameters we estimated include the mean and standard deviation of the taste distribution, the location parameter of the shock distribution, and the discount factor. We also estimated an adjustment to mean taste in the early years of the teaching career, as discussed in Chapter Six. We emphasize that the model was estimated from actual data and is not calibrated. Calibration would select parameter values from a sequence of guesses that depend on model fit under prior guesses, whereas estimation finds the parameters that simultaneously maximize the model's fit to the data and provides standard errors of the estimates by which to judge their statistical significance.

The model's parameters were estimated by maximum likelihood, where Equation 4.11 gives the likelihood function. Optimization is done using the BFGS (Broyden-Fletcher-Goldfarb-Shanno) algorithm, a standard hill-climbing method. Standard errors of the estimates were computed by numerically differentiating the likelihood function at the maximum point to yield a Hessian matrix, and then by taking the square root of the absolute value of the diagonal of the inverse of this Hessian matrix.

To compute the likelihood function in Equation 4.11, it is necessary to evaluate the integral in $\mathcal{L}_i$, i.e., to integrate out the unobserved heterogeneity in taste for teaching employment in CPS. We did this by computing the average over a set of 23 points sampled from the current trial population distribution of taste.[11] For each sample taste, the dynamic program was solved for each individual, and the likelihood value for that individual was computed. We integrated over the distribution of tastes by taking the average of the likelihoods over the 23 sample points.

The process of estimation tries different trial values of the parameters until the career likelihoods are maximized for the sample of teachers used. While this is the standard approach in maximum-likelihood estimation, the computational burden associated with the DRM occurs

---

[11]   We constructed the sample by scaling a 23-point standard normal Halton sequence using the trial values of the population mean and standard deviation of taste.

because for each trial set of parameters, the dynamic programming problem has to be re-solved for all periods for all 23 draws of taste. Then, given the new solution, the choice probabilities are updated, and the likelihood function is reevaluated to determine whether the fit has improved and in what direction the next trial parameters should be changed to improve it in the next iteration. Re-solving the dynamic program requires extensive computation for each individual in the data.

To judge goodness of fit, we used the parameter estimates to simulate retention rates by year of service of teachers and compared those rates with the actual data. We show goodness-of-fit diagrams in Chapter Six when we present the model parameter estimates.

Conclusion

The DRM developed in this chapter is an adaptation of the military DRM to the education setting. Although teaching and military service are very different, many features of the compensation systems in the two settings are similar, and the DRM is flexible enough to capture key factors that enter teachers' retention decisions. The model incorporates the financial incentives associated with the lifetime stream of salary income and future retirement benefits associated with teaching. A model of retention in which teachers could respond to only current period income would miss the potential effects of retirement benefits, a large component of teachers' compensation, on retention earlier in the career. The model also incorporates a "taste" for teaching in CPS, recognizing that teachers' decisions to continue teaching in Chicago may be determined in part by a preference for teaching over other occupations, the working conditions in their schools, or other nonpecuniary benefits associated with teaching. In the following chapters, we discuss the data inputs necessary to estimate the model and then discuss the model estimates and evaluate the simulation results.

CHAPTER FIVE

Chicago Teacher Retention Data and Teacher and Nonteacher Wage Profiles

---

Chicago Teacher Retention Data

Data on Chicago Public School teachers come from the Teacher Service Record (TSR) database of the ISBE. The TSR data contain annual school-year censuses of public school teachers for the years 1979 to 2012. The data include a unique identifier for each teacher, which allows us to create a teacher-level retention profile for each teacher. We use the data to identify entering cohorts of teachers and observe teacher age, total creditable years of service, breaks in service, salary, and exit from teaching in Chicago. With the data we can determine eligibility for future retirement benefits and benefit level, conditional on the retention paths a teacher might choose given her current state as defined by age, years of service, and personal preference for teaching. Although we focus on teacher retention in Chicago, the TSR data include additional variables that could be useful in future work, for instance, the teacher's level of education, the school at which a teacher is working, and whether, after leaving the Chicago system, the teacher enters another school district in Illinois.

We analyze CPS teacher retention for teachers aged 22 to 30 when they entered CPS. These teachers presumably had little or no prior teaching experience. Over our data period, 1979 to 2012, the total population of teachers in the Chicago district was around 20,000 each year. It was 18,887 in 1979, ranged from 20,000 to 23,000 in most years from 1980 to 2012, and was 22,435 in 2012. The portion of the population contained in our sample, teachers entering at ages 22 to 30, stood at 10,000 to 11,000 in most years, or about 45 to 50 percent of the total population of teachers.[1] The remaining 50 to 55 percent of teachers entered laterally by transferring from other districts, entered teaching after 30, or reentered the Chicago system after a gap of more than two years. We included in our sample those with gaps of two years or less under the assumption that short gaps are typically for approved absences, e.g., for further education or family reasons.

Figure 5.1 displays cumulative percentage retained of entering teacher cohorts (aged 22 to 30 at entry) to each year of service. The red curve is for those entering between 1979 and 2000. The first year, 1979, is the earliest year in our data when we can directly observe entry. We "closed" the entry window in 2000 to allow 12 years for following teachers; 2012 is the last year on which we have observations. The blue curve is for teachers entering between 1992 and 2000.

Figure 5.1
Chicago Public School Teacher Retention for Those Entering at Ages 22 to 30

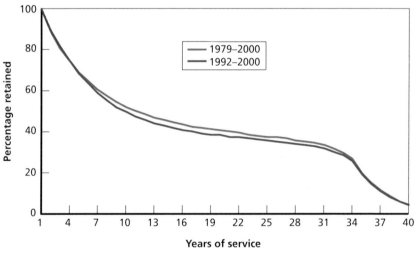

RAND RR1448-5.1

---

[1]   The count decreased to 8,000 to 9,000 in 2007 to 2012 because of a decline in hiring. This was the period of the great recession, and incumbent teachers were unlikely to exit, given fewer alternative job possibilities.

Because the period of observation ends in 2012, a teacher entering in 1979 is observed for 34 years, while teachers entering in 1992 to 2000 are observed for 13 to 20 years, and retention beyond that is imputed based on continuation rates from the full sample of entrants, 1979 to 2000. As seen, the retention curves are similar though not identical up to 20 years of service. The curves are 3 to 4 percentage points different from years of service 10 to 20. The somewhat lower retention of the more recent entrants may reflect school closures (Chapter Three). In both curves, about one-third of the teachers complete at least 30 years of service, and retention at year 34 is 26 percent. Year 34 is when the retirement benefit multiplier reaches its maximum, 75 percent, and retention declines rapidly from there on.

By using teacher age and years of service for incumbent teachers in 1979, we can also infer whether a teacher entered in an earlier year than 1979 and was aged 22 to 30 at entry. We use this insight in constructing an estimation sample that includes incumbents. The estimation sample combines teachers who entered CPS in years 1992 to 2000 and were aged 22 to 30 at entry, along with incumbent teachers in 1992 who entered CPS in an earlier year and were aged 22 to 30 at entry. For teachers entering from 1979 to 1991, we know the exact year of entry; for instance, teachers entering (and present) in 1979 and retained continuously would be in their 14th year of service in 1992. For teachers continuously present from 1979 to 1992 and in their 15th or higher year in 1992, we use age and years of service in their 1979 record to infer their year of entry and age at entry. If their age at entry was in the range of 22 to 30, they were included in the sample.

Table 5.1 provides summary statistics for each component of our estimation sample, 1992 to 2000 entrants (who were age 22 to 30 at entry into CPS) and 1992 incumbent teachers (who were age 22 to 30 at entry into CPS). Statistics for all CPS entry cohorts from 1979 to 2000 are presented for comparison. We considered using an estimation sample consisting of all entry cohorts from 1979 to 2000, who have very similar characteristics to the 1992 to 2000 entry cohorts, but even with early-year cohorts, e.g., 1979 to 1985, the teachers did not have enough years of service by 2012 to observe their retirement behavior. As an alternative, we created the mixed sample of 1992 to

Table 5.1
Summary Statistics for Teacher Entry Cohorts and Incumbents Data

Characteristic	Cohorts 1979–2000		Cohorts 1992–2000		Incumbents in 1992	
	Mean	Std. Dev	Mean	Std. Dev	Mean	Std. Dev.
Years of service in Illinois	12.73	8.25	10.71	6.16	30.79	7.51
Years of service in Chicago	11.45	8.44	9.49	6.32	30.47	7.93
Position at career start						
High school	0.15	0.36	0.17	0.38	0.18	0.39
Elementary/middle school	0.69	0.46	0.71	0.45	0.60	0.49
Special education	0.16	0.36	0.12	0.32	0.19	0.39
Position at last observation						
High school teacher	0.15	0.35	0.17	0.37	0.17	0.38
Elementary/middle school teacher	0.59	0.49	0.63	0.48	0.50	0.50
Special education teacher	0.13	0.34	0.09	0.29	0.18	0.38
District/school leader[b]	0.07	0.25	0.06	0.23	0.07	0.26
Ever worked charter school	0.01	0.09	0.00	0.06	0.00	0.03
Age[a]	26.08	2.11	26.10	2.09	40.98	6.16
Female	0.81	0.39	0.80	0.40	0.77	0.42
White, non-Hispanic	0.51	0.50	0.56	0.50	0.43	0.50
Black, non-Hispanic	0.26	0.44	0.22	0.41	0.47	0.50
Hispanic	0.17	0.38	0.18	0.38	0.08	0.28

Table 5.1—Continued

Characteristic	Cohorts 1979–2000		Cohorts 1992–2000		Incumbents in 1992	
	Mean	Std. Dev	Mean	Std. Dev	Mean	Std. Dev.
Educated in Illinois	0.72	0.45	0.69	0.46	0.78	0.41
Degree[a]						
B.A.	0.90	0.31	0.88	0.32	0.59	0.49
M.A.+	0.10	0.30	0.11	0.32	0.41	0.49
Degree at last observation						
B.A.	0.43	0.49	0.42	0.49	0.36	0.48
M.A.+	0.57	0.50	0.58	0.49	0.64	0.48
N unique educators	7,684		4,867		5,622	
N unique educators stay in Chicago	6,541		4,087		5,391	

[a]Age is average age at entry for the entering cohorts of 1979–2000 and 1992–2000 and average age in 1992 for incumbent teachers in 1992. This is similarly true for degree.

[b]School leaders include superintendents, assistant superintendents, principals, assistant principals, and directors.

2000 entrants plus 1992 incumbent teachers. A major advantage of this sample is that many of the incumbents reached retirement eligibility by 2012.

The 1992 to 2000 entrants had 9.49 years of service in CPS and 10.71 years in Illinois as of 2012. Some CPS entrants who later leave CPS enter other Illinois school districts, adding to their years of service. Also, years of service are right-censored in 2012, and this affects mean years of service reported in the table; however, the estimation code of the DRM accounts for right censoring, so it does not bias the model estimates. As seen, the means and standard deviations of the 1979 to 2000 cohorts and the 1992 to 2000 cohorts are similar for all variables apart from years of service, which is higher in the 1979 to 2000 sample because it follows teachers for more years.

In the 1992 to 2000 entry cohorts, 17 percent were high school teachers at entry, 71 percent were elementary and middle school teachers, and 12 percent were special education teachers. At the teachers' last observation, some teachers had moved to supervisory positions, e.g., 6 percent were in school or district leadership positions. Eighty percent of the entrants were female, and the average age of entrants was 26. Fifty-six percent of the entrants were white non-Hispanic, 22 percent were black non-Hispanic, and 18 percent were Hispanic. Most of the teachers, 69 percent, were educated in Illinois.

At entry, 88 percent of the teachers had a bachelor's degree and 11 percent had a master's degree or higher. By the last observation, 42 percent had a bachelor's, and 58 percent had a master's or higher. The large increase in the percentage with a master's degree may be a response to the teacher salary schedule. A master's degree added approximately $4,000 per year to a teacher's salary.[2] The higher salary also means a higher final average salary, hence higher retirement benefits. Based on the means in Table 5.1, a typical salary trajectory starts with a teacher entering at the bachelor's level. Many teachers then add to their education, and about 60 percent of the teachers with 20 or more years of service have a master's degree or higher.

The 1992 incumbents are the cross-section of teachers in that year with years of service ranging from one to 40, and mean years of service as of 2012 were 30.47 in CPS and 30.79 years in Illinois. The 1992 incumbents were on average 41 years old in 1992, 77 percent were female, 78 percent were educated in Illinois, 59 percent had a bachelor's degree, and 41 percent had a master's or higher. At the last observation, 36 percent had a bachelor's, and 64 percent had a master's or higher. The increase in the percentage with master's degrees suggests that even veteran teachers had an incentive to obtain a master's degree.

---

[2]   The salary data are for 208-day positions for the 2014–2015 school year and appear in Appendix A: Part 1 of the Chicago Teachers Union contract (CTU undated[a]). The starting salary for a teacher with a bachelor's degree was $50,653, climbing to $84,658 after 15 years. The starting salary for a teacher with a master's degree was $54,161, rising to $88,272 after 15 years with a master's.

Teacher and Nonteacher Earnings by Age

The earnings of teachers in the Chicago Public Schools relative to alternative employment options can affect teacher retention decisions. To capture this financial incentive, we develop empirical estimates of earnings by age (earnings profiles) for CPS teachers and observationally similar nonteachers.

Chicago Teacher Earnings Profile

We estimated the Chicago teacher earnings with the salary information from the TSR data. We used this information to generate cross-sectional earnings profiles from 1979–2012. We estimated an ordinary least squares regression with a piecewise linear specification in years of service interacted with degree level, bachelor's or master's. We did this separately for each year and included only full-time teachers in the sample. The regression fit the data well, as expected from earnings data based on salary schedules and stable progression through the schedules. The r-squared was above 0.70 in 90 percent of the years and always above 0.50. Further details are in Appendix B.

We used the cross-sectional earnings profiles to create earnings profiles by teachers' entry cohort. For a given entry cohort Y, first-year earnings came from predicted earnings for the first year of service in the year Y cross-sectional pay profile, second-year earnings came from predicted earnings in the second year of service in the year Y+1 cross-sectional pay profile, and so on until the individual reached 34 years of service or fiscal year 2012, the last observed year. Earnings after 2012 were projected using the nearest cohort's earnings growth for the unobserved years of service (in terms of age).[3] All earnings were discounted to 2013 dollars using the annual averages for the consumer price index-urban (CPI-U) of the Bureau of Labor Statistics.

---

[3]   We estimate the teacher earnings regressions in terms of years of service rather than age because the TSR data include years of service information. However, we do not have years of service information in the Current Population Survey used to estimate the nonteacher earnings profile, so we use age instead, as discussed below. To put both profiles in the same units, the predicted earnings profile for teachers is expressed in terms of age rather than years of service.

The blue line in Figure 5.2 shows the predicted earnings profile a teacher might expect if she taught in Chicago public schools throughout her career. Earnings increase rapidly in the first 20 years of the career—the first half—then taper off to virtually no increase over the second half of the career. Needless to say, the defined benefit retirement system provides senior teachers with a powerful incentive to continue teaching until reaching normal retirement age.[4]

Chicago Nonteacher Earnings Profile

To capture the salaries associated with teachers' outside employment options, we use data from the Current Population Survey. This is a

Figure 5.2
Internal and External Earnings Profiles for Chicago Teachers, by Age

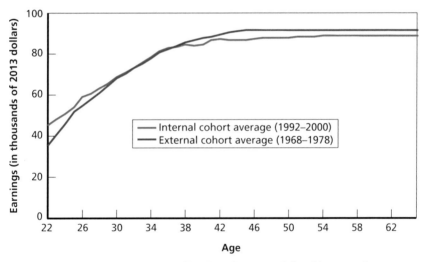

NOTES: For the internal earnings profile, the cohorts are defined by year of entry to teaching in CPS. For the external earnings profile, the cohorts are defined by year of birth. The birth cohorts selected capture the alternative earnings profiles of teachers in their 20s to early 30s who entered teaching in Chicago in 1992–2000.
RAND RR1448-5.2

---

[4]   In addition to salary and pension benefits, CPS also offers health insurance to teachers while they are working and retiree health insurance benefits (with some restrictions). These benefits and others were not incorporated into the model.

monthly survey of about 60,000 households conducted by the Bureau of the Census for the Bureau of Labor Statistics. It is designed to be representative of the population at the national, state, and large metropolitan area levels. It collects detailed information on labor earnings and demographic characteristics, including age and residential location.

The Current Population Survey (1962–2014) was used to construct teachers' expected earnings profiles for non-CPS employment. We estimated a Tobit model that allows earnings to vary by year, birth-cohort, educational attainment, metropolitan location (and separately by the Chicago metropolitan area), and accounts for the top-coding of high earners in our data. The model estimates were applied to the sample of individuals working in the Chicago metropolitan area with a bachelor's degree to predict the earnings profiles. Further details of this analysis are in Appendix B.

The red line in Figure 5.2 shows the estimated earnings profile for full-time workers in the Chicago metropolitan area who are not in teaching. We freeze earnings at age 45, as the model would otherwise predict an earnings decrease. The predicted decrease results from selection out of working at older ages. The earnings profile in age is very similar to that for teaching in CPS. The starting salary for a young worker is lower in nonteaching positions but grows at a faster rate. It flattens out about five years later than the teacher profile, resulting in higher earnings for workers in their mid-30s and older.

Conclusion

In this chapter we described key data inputs required to estimate the DRM developed in Chapter Four, namely, our estimation sample of CPS teachers and the salary profiles associated with teaching in CPS and with external employment. The estimation sample includes entering CPS teachers in years 1992–2000 who were age 22–30 at entry and incumbent teachers observed teaching in CPS in 1992 who were also age 22–30 when they began teaching. The teachers are followed longitudinally to 2012, the last year of sample data. The similarity between the retention profiles and the characteristics of teachers who started teaching before 1992 and those who entered between 1992 and 2000 supports the use of the combined sample of incumbent and entering teachers in the estimation. The combined sample provides better coverage of retention over the full career. The empirical retention profile exhibits characteristics observed in other contexts where the DRM has been successfully utilized, specifically high early-career attrition and increased attrition at retirement eligibility. The earnings profiles are also in line with previous work and our expectations; salaries grow steadily for younger workers and flatten out around middle age, with teachers earning more than nonteachers very early in their careers and somewhat less later. These empirical observations suggest that the DRM developed in Chapter Four is appropriate to model the retention decisions of Chicago teachers. In the next chapter, we discuss the model estimates and evaluate how well the model fits the observed retention profile.

CHAPTER SIX

DRM Parameter Estimates and Model Fit

Exploring Model Specification

We began model estimation with the basic four-parameter specification of the DRM that includes the mean and standard deviation of taste, the standard deviation of the shock, and the personal discount factor. But we found that this specification did not fit the observed data as well as we would like, so we explored alternative specifications and found one that fit well. This chapter first discusses model specification and presents two graphics of model fit, then discusses the parameter estimates of the preferred specification.

Figure 6.1 shows the fit of the basic four-parameter DRM, called model 1, and the fit of the preferred specification, called model 2. Teacher retention predicted from model 1 is too low in early years of service, too high in years 8 to 30, and too low from 30 to about 35 years. Thus, model 1 had difficulty capturing two key empirical facts: a more gradual decline in teacher retention over the first ten years, and retirement at 34 years of service, the point at which retirement benefits hit their maximum.

Finding a specification that fit well proved challenging. We estimated model 1 on a sample limited to entrants between 1992 and 2000 and found that its predicted retention fit well in early years of service but was too high after 34 years of service. We inferred that this was caused by selection: The mean taste conditional on remaining to 34 years was so high that teachers did not sufficiently respond to retirement incentives. The results suggested that a high mean taste was needed in early years to sustain early-career retention but led to

Figure 6.1
Observed and Predicted Teacher Retention

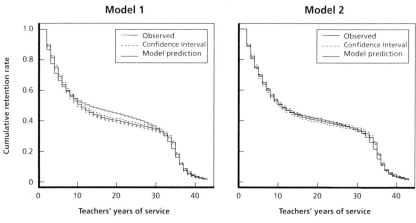

too high a mean taste conditional on staying late into a teaching career. Further, when we estimated model 1 on the sample of teachers attaining 20 years of service in 1992 to 2000, it fit late-career retention well. This suggested that estimated taste conditional on 20 years of service allowed accurate responsiveness to pension incentives. Together, these exploratory estimations suggested that taste for teaching evolved with experience and, in particular, had a temporarily high value in the initial years of teaching.

In view of this, we added an early-career taste factor to model 1 to create model 2. This allowed taste to be high at the beginning of the career and decline as years of service increased. A specification that worked well assumes a linear reduction in this factor over the first 12 years of service, equal to $\max\left\{\psi - \frac{\psi}{12} \times Years\ of\ Service, 0\right\}$. The parameter Ψ is estimated. In the first year of service, the amount $\frac{11}{12}\psi$ is added to each teacher's taste, and in the 11th year of service $\frac{1}{12}\psi$ is added. The factor is zero at 12 years of service, and at that time taste reverts to a teacher's persistent mean taste. As Figure 6.1 shows, model 2 fits the data well. It follows the initial decline in retention or, stated differently, the higher attrition among early-career teachers. It also fits the decrease in retention at 34 years of service well.

Still, the predicted decrease in retention in years 34 and 35 is somewhat larger than observed. We think this could reflect an artifact of constructing teacher years of experience. About 20 percent of teachers were absent from CPS for a year or two and returned. We gave these teachers years-of-service credit for the absent years. Thus, some teachers who appear to have 34 years of service in fact had 33 or 32 years, which would make the "observed" retention curve in Figure 6.1 descend later than it should. It is possible that the model's prediction of lower retention than observed at 34 and 35 may be accurate.

As part of our exploratory work, we considered a number of alternatives to model 2. One alternative included a gradual decrease of 1 percent per year or, alternatively, one and a half percent per year, in external earnings as years of teaching increased. This was motivated by the idea that teachers may accumulate specific human capital not transferable to other employment, and, if so, additional years may not improve nonteaching employment options. Another alternative was a greater taste for leisure in old age. This was a variant of the adjustment used by Ni and Podgursky (2015). Operationally, we included a linear and quadratic cost to teaching after age 50. A third alternative included involuntary separations in which the likelihood of separation was higher earlier in the career. This was motivated by lower job security among pretenure teachers. But this did not improve the fit of the model. In fact, empirically there is little change in the retention probability around the tenure mark. A fourth alternative was a nonlinear version of the early-career adjustment factor. We found model 2 to be superior to these alternatives in terms of fit and the value of the maximized likelihood and, as such, is our preferred model.

We also chose to omit own–Social Security benefits from the calculation of the DRM value function. Teachers are not covered by Social Security but could qualify for these benefits as a result of moving into the covered sector when they leave teaching or before they start teaching. We do not model or have data on the teacher's retirement from the labor force, i.e., the decision to stop working entirely. Rather, we assume that work life ends at age 66, and teachers collect the present discounted value of their pension at this time if they have not yet exited teaching. We considered including Social Security benefits, but this led to an important complication. Social Security benefits require a minimum of 40 quarters of contribution. This requirement can interact with the assumed length of work life to create potential focal points for exit. For example, if we chose a maximum work life age of 66 and included years between 22 and entry into teaching as Social Security contributing years, then we would be assuming that a teacher would have to leave at the 34th year of service to satisfy the minimum 10 years to qualify for Social Security benefits (e.g., a 26-year-old entrant would have 4 creditable years, ages 22 to 26, before teaching, and 6 creditable years after teaching, ages 60 to 66). We found that including Social Security benefits produced poorer fit and was sensitive to the choice of maximum working age. It is possible that many teachers never pursue a nonteaching career after qualifying for their pension, that they have insignificant earnings records to qualify, or that the expected Social Security benefits are too small to justify the effort. We view this as an open question for future research.

Discussion of Parameter Estimates

The parameter estimates for models 1 and 2 are given in Table 6.1 along with standard errors and z-scores. All of the parameter estimates for both models are statistically significant. The parameters for the mean and standard deviation of taste, shock scale, and early-career taste factor are denominated in thousands of dollars.

The parameter estimates from model 2 indicate that teachers, on average, have a strong preference for teaching—equivalent to about $49,700 at the beginning of the second year of teaching (this value is computed as $\mu + \frac{11}{12}\psi$).[1] The CPS starting salary in 2013 was about $49,000, so starting taste was about equal to starting salary. The salary plus the taste totaled nearly $100,000, and in addition to this the teacher received the discounted value of the option to choose between

---

[1] The beginning of the second potential year of teaching represents a teacher's first decision period. We assume the teacher must complete the first year in order to be counted as an entrant. Also, note that this value may differ slightly from the value presented in Figure 6.2 due to the usage of Halton sequences for numerical integration.

Table 6.1
Parameter Estimates and Standard Errors

Parameter	Model 1			Model 2		
	Estimate	Standard Error	z-score	Estimate	Standard Error	z-score
Taste						
Mean	15.70	0.56	28.04	−8.61	1.44	−5.98
Standard deviation	32.08	0.64	50.13	49.78	1.17	42.55
Shock scale	97.51	1.76	55.40	68.29	1.61	42.42
Personal discount factor						
Untransformed[a]	2.60	0.003	866.67	2.86	0.0331	86.40
Transformed	0.931			0.946		
Early-career taste factor	n.a.			69.42	3.01	23.06

[a] In estimating the personal discount factor, we transform the factor using a logit function to bound it between zero and one.

teaching and nonteaching in the next period, plus a shock that could be either positive or negative.

A positive mean taste for teaching in CPS is consistent with teacher pay being less than nonteaching alternatives except very early in a teacher's career. The nonpecuniary aspects represented by taste are a major reason for teachers to stay in teaching. The aspects may be a work schedule permitting a summer break; the ability to have approved absences in service for raising children or taking care of family members; the intrinsic satisfaction from teaching, e.g., ability to have a major influence on students' lives; or other sources. The linear decrease in the taste factor could reflect declining satisfaction from teaching, unexpectedly high effort needed for class preparation, burdensome record keeping, or the time required to address the issues of individual students, e.g., those with individualized study plans or perhaps with disciplinary or family issues. Teaching may provide high nonpecuniary benefits for teachers in their first few years of teaching that reflect the new experience of influencing a child's life. Over time, the taste for teaching may decline as classes become repetitive, a teacher recognizes recurring difficulties in the classroom, or, simply, the impact on students' lives becomes routine. These are speculations consistent with the literature that finds relatively high attrition in the early years of teaching. High early attrition occurs despite the possibility of transferring within a large district from the teacher's school at entry, which might not be the teacher's preferred school, to a different school more in line with preferences.

The mean taste represents the average mean taste of an entering cohort of teachers in the CPS. As the entry cohort progresses through its career, some teachers who were a part of the entry cohort will exit teaching to pursue other opportunities. The mean taste of those who remain will increase, not because individual tastes change over time in our model, but because those with lower taste are less likely to stay. Mean taste among retained teachers evolves because of the selective retention on persistent taste and the decrease in the early taste factor. Figure 6.2 shows the mean taste conditional on retention to a specific year of service based on model 2. The conditional mean taste for teaching is never negative, implying those teachers who remain in teaching

Figure 6.2
Conditional Mean of the Taste Distribution, by Year of Service

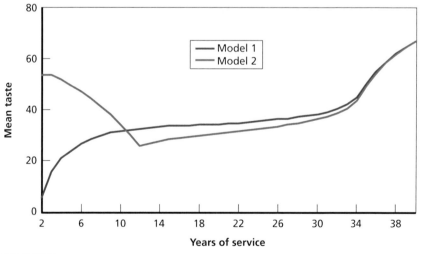

receive a positive nonpecuniary reward from teaching. Also, although conditional mean taste declines during the first years of teaching, it increases at 34 years of service. This is caused by the retirement of teachers, and only teachers with the highest taste for teaching stay in teaching. Their high taste compensates for the forgone receipt of retirement benefits.

There is significant variation in the taste for teaching. The standard deviation is $49,780, implying diverse taste at entry into teaching. In our modeling, this variation comes entirely from variation in permanent taste, while transitory taste is the same for all teachers in a given year of teaching and decreases from entry until vanishing at year 12. Figures 6.3 and 6.4 display the taste distribution. Figure 6.3 shows the distribution of permanent taste, and as seen the variance of taste decreases as years of service increase. Retained teachers become more homogeneous over time, with most of the decrease in variance occurring by 20 years of teaching. Also, the mean permanent taste increases as years of service increase. It starts at a negative value, −$8,610 (see

Figure 6.3
Distribution of Permanent Taste, by Year of Service (YOS)

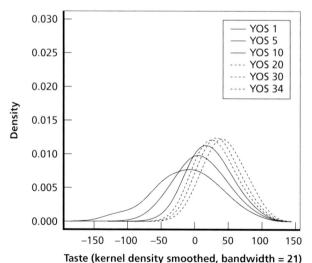

Taste (kernel density smoothed, bandwidth = 21)

RAND RR1448-6.3

Figure 6.4
Distribution of Permanent and Transitory Taste, by
Year of Service

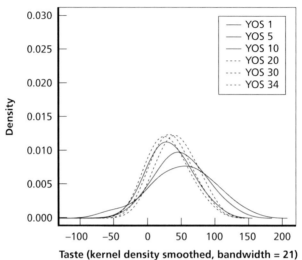

RAND RR1448-6.4

Table 6.1), and increases to about $25,000 by year 30. But when transitory taste is included (Figure 6.4), mean taste decreases over the 12 years, is slightly lower at year 20 than at year 10, and then increases, consistent with Figure 6.2.

The estimate of the location parameter of the shock distribution is 68.29 in model 2. (The mean of the shock parameter is zero in our implementation of the DRM.) The standard deviation of the shock is $\pi\lambda/\sqrt{6}$ times this amount, or $87,580. To put this in perspective, a teacher with 11 years of service in school year 2012–2013 had a salary just above $70,000 and a mean taste of about $30,420 (Figure 6.2). The teacher would also value the opportunity to choose between teaching and nonteaching in the next year. This teacher, then, could face a negative teaching shock of more than a standard deviation of the shock distribution, or a positive external shock of the same magnitude, and would choose to remain in teaching. (For comparison, recall that Ni and Podgursky's shock variance was nearly two times the value of the utility of teaching at age 55 [Chapter Three].)

The estimate of the personal discount factor is 0.9457, implying that someone would trade $100 in compensation next year for $94.57 in current compensation. The personal discount factor is equivalent to a personal discount rate of 5.74 percent. This is higher than the rate estimated by Ni and Podgursky (2015) of 3.5 percent. Their sample, however, was limited to teachers 47 to 58 years old in the first year of their sample, whereas ours consists of teachers who began their CPS teaching career at ages 22 to 30. Perhaps the personal discount rate declines with age at younger ages. We have assumed no change with age. Allowing for change with age as well as heterogeneity in the discount rate across individuals are topics for future work.

Conclusion

Overall, model 2 nicely fits teacher retention over the entire career. The estimates indicate that teachers find a significant nonpecuniary benefit to teaching, and this benefit varies widely by individual and years of service. Its mean value evolves over the career yet is positive in all years, providing a buffer against negative shocks. We found that model fit depended on the presence of an early-career taste factor. It is possible that other specifications would also fit, but the alternatives we tried did not work as well. We have not identified the elements of the teaching environment or experience that give rise to this factor, though we have listed some possibilities that correspond to issues addressed in the literature. The decrease in this factor over the first years of teaching is consistent with higher attrition early in the career. The phenomenon of its decrease is also consistent with educators' emphasis on the importance of induction and mentoring programs to prepare teachers for the array of challenges they will face. These programs may be seen as a way of setting more accurate initial expectations and providing teachers with locally relevant skills and knowledge to work effectively in their classrooms and in the school. They may thereby serve to set a more accurate initial value of early-career taste and decrease its rate of decline.

CHAPTER SEVEN

Policy Simulations

The DRM has been used in several settings to simulate the effects of a change in current or deferred compensation on the ability to retain an existing workforce, namely the active and reserve component of the U.S. military, as well as the federal civil service. In this chapter, we use the estimated parameters of model 2 to assess the effect of a change in current or future compensation on CPS teacher retention. We note that the policy simulations reflect the response of existing teachers in CPS and do not incorporate any changes to entering teacher cohorts that may result from the policy changes.[1] The specific estimates should not be assumed to apply to other districts; however, the qualitative direction and rough magnitude of responsiveness may be of broader interest.

We consider seven types of compensation changes, listed following, some of which modify current CPS compensation, while others modify deferred compensation through the pension. The purpose of these simulations is to demonstrate the new capability we have developed as a result of the estimated DRM for teachers rather than to

---

[1] A change in CPS compensation could affect the pool of applicant teachers. For instance, we expect that a decrease in CPS compensation would decrease the supply of applicants. An individual at the margin of applying would decide not to apply, and this decision would result from the relatively lower CPS compensation compared to compensation elsewhere, and not because of a change in the individual's taste for teaching. However, given the decrease in CPS compensation, individuals who exit the pool of applicants would tend to have a lower taste for teaching compared with those who remain in the pool. There could also be an effect on teacher quality, e.g., if higher-quality teachers also have better opportunities in nonteaching jobs, the decrease in CPS occupations might induce some higher-quality teachers to exit the application pool.

address any specific policy. However, the compensation changes we examine are related to recent policy changes, including the 2011 pension reforms, as well as policies that might be contemplated in the future. For each compensation change, we compare the new simulated retention profile to the no-reform, status quo retention profile to demonstrate the effect of the reform. In practice, the simulated retention profiles associated with various compensation changes could instead be compared to a school district's desired retention profile.

Current Compensation

- A 3-percent reduction in current teacher pay
- A retention bonus after five years.

Deferred Compensation

- An increase in the vesting, early, full-benefit collection ages (reflective of the 2011 pension reforms)
- A decrease in COLA (reflective of the 2011 pension reforms)
- Extending the number of years used in calculating the high pay in the pension formula (reflective of the 2011 pension reforms)
- Decreased multiplier (reduction in the pension multiplier from 2.2 percent to 1 percent)
- 2011 pension system reforms.

Changes in Current Compensation

Severe budget constraints and state constitutional limitations on adjusting previously defined pension benefits have placed renewed interest on changes to current compensation, namely in the form of pay cuts. Every few years, the CTU and the CPS system negotiate a contract that includes provisions affecting salary.

We consider the possibility that real pay permanently decreases by 3 percent, which could be accomplished by a pay cut or over time through a pay freeze. Consequently, the nonteaching alternative job will look more appealing because teacher pay is relatively lower. Additionally, because a teacher's pension is determined, in part, by her highest four years of nominal earnings while teaching, her pension would be lower as a result of a decrease in current pay. Therefore, teacher retention should fall. Because of the unambiguous theoretical effects of a pay decrease, in terms of both current and deferred compensations, a pay cut policy experiment can help provide an indication of how many teachers are on the margin between staying and leaving, where a small change in compensation would induce them to leave.

Figure 7.1 presents the steady-state retention results of a 3-percent across-the-board decrease in salary. By steady state, we mean that a teacher would spend his or her entire career under a salary system that was lower by 3 percent at every year of service. We assume no change in the number of teachers hired, so the results show the effects on retention only. We find that teachers would provide 0.725 fewer years of ser-

Figure 7.1
Simulated Steady-State Retention Effect of a 3-Percent Decrease in Current CPS Teacher Salary

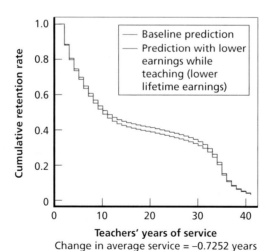

Change in average service = –0.7252 years
Change in force size = –4.322 percent

RAND *RR1448-7.1*

vice, on average, to CPS, which amounts to a 4.32-percent decrease in years of service over an entry cohort's CPS career. An alternative way to understand the significance of this value is that in 1992, 10,485 teachers were between ages 22 and 30 at entry, and we estimate that with no changes, they would each provide an average of 16.82 years of teaching to CPS. A 3-percent reduction in their salary would cause the average to decrease to 16.09 years of teaching. To maintain the same expected total years of teaching that the 1992 entrants and incumbent teachers were expected to provide, approximately 472 new teachers would need to be hired at entry. As demonstrated in Figure 7.1, changes in the exit rate from service occur between one and five years of service, leading to a lower level of retention from year five through year 30. The literature finds that teacher effectiveness improves rapidly in the first few years of teaching, and the 3-percent salary reduction would cause a greater loss of teachers through that phase. This, in turn, would mean fewer fully productive teachers for the next 20 years of service. Later policy action might react to this loss by seeking to hire mid-career teachers from other districts, but an attempt to do so would raise the question of which teachers, and what quality of teacher, would be willing to accept CPS's lower salary schedule.

Policymakers could consider an alternative mechanism successful in the retention of officer and enlisted service members in the U.S. military: a continuation bonus. A continuation bonus is given to an individual at some milestone of service. In our simulations, we test the effect of a $10,000 bonus given to teachers who complete five years of service in CPS. The aim of this policy would be to help reduce the 50-percent attrition by the tenth year. In conjunction with a change in pension benefits, a continuation bonus would provide a method by which deferred compensation could be substituted in favor of current compensation—which, unlike deferred compensation, is not discounted by the individual.

Figure 7.2 presents the results from a $10,000 continuation bonus after five years of service. We observe a small positive retention effect from the continuation bonus, with a slight increase before and after the bonus period. The ineffectiveness of the continuation bonus is reflective of the significant distribution in nonpecuniary taste to teach. Most

Figure 7.2
Simulated Steady-State Retention Effects of
a $10,000 Continuation Bonus at Five Years
of Service

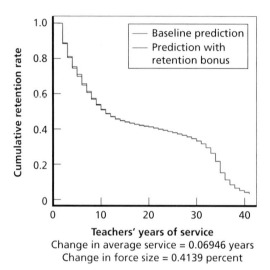

Teachers' years of service
Change in average service = 0.06946 years
Change in force size = 0.4139 percent

RAND RR1448-7.2

of the reduction in the first 10 years of teaching is a consequence of individuals with a low taste for teaching being sorted out. While a continuation bonus after five years might keep some people in teaching for a short period of time, it is not effective as a mechanism of keeping them in teaching in the long term. Perhaps a higher bonus coupled with a payback feature would be more effective. [2]

_____

[2]   The $10,000 continuation bonus does not have an obligation of service or a payback feature if the teacher leaves before the end of the obligation. These features could be added, however. For instance, the bonus might be $30,000 paid over three years and with a three-year commitment to stay, in which case leaving early forfeits the next bonus payment; or it could be paid as a lump sum up front but with a pro rata payback for early exit.

Changes in Deferred Compensation

Defined benefit pensions represent the primary form of deferred compensation for teachers. In the past two years, many Illinois policymakers, including the Illinois legislature, the governor's office, and the Chicago mayor, have put forward proposals to reshape both current and former pension benefits. The Illinois State Constitution states that "membership in any pension or retirement system of the State, [...] shall be an enforceable contractual relationship, the benefits of which shall not be diminished or impaired." Laws that have been passed by the legislature in the past two years that have altered past or current benefits have not been upheld in court, with state courts ruling, based on the state constitution, that accrued benefits cannot be reduced. This has placed policymakers in a conundrum as they face growing budget demands due to an underfunded pension fund. The only legally and politically successful policy changes to date have been altering the benefits of new hires. While this is not a solution to the more immediate fiscal challenges from existing pension obligations, it may improve the financial security of the pension obligations due to new CPS entrants (although nothing legally precludes using this funding to cover current obligations and, judging from the past, there still may be uncertainty over whether the reduced benefits of new entrants will be fully funded). In this section we consider four changes to deferred compensation:

1. an increase in the age at which a teacher vests, the earliest age at which a vested teacher may begin collecting benefits, and the age at which a teacher can collect unreduced benefits
2. a decrease in the COLA from being set equal to the consumer price index (CPI) to the minimum of 3 percent or one-half of the CPI
3. changing the pension benefit from being based on the highest four years of nominal earnings to being based on the highest eight years of nominal earnings
4. a reduction in the pension multiplier from 2.2 percent to 1 percent.

The first three policy variations reflect part of the changes imposed on new CPS entrants hired after 2010. We conduct the policy simulations not because this is a policy actively under consideration, although it could be with a constitutional amendment, but because it is indicative of the likely retention impact on new hires after 2010. The validity of this experiment relies on the assumption that the post-2010 entry cohorts are similar to the 1992–2000 entrant cohorts and 1992 incumbents.

As part of the reforms to pensions of new hires after 2010, referred to as Tier 2 pensions, a CPS employee vests in his or her pension at the completion of ten years of service instead of five years. In addition, the earliest a CPS employee can begin collecting a pension is age 62, whereas a Tier 1 (pre-2011 hire) CPS employee could begin collecting as early as age 55 with 20 years of service. Finally, the age at which a CPS employee can begin collecting an unreduced pension is 67, whereas a Tier 1 CPS employee could begin collecting an unreduced benefit as early as age 55 with at least 34 years of service, 60 with at least 20 years of service, or 62 with at least five years of service. We allow the pension formula to reflect these differences and simulate the consequences of these new rules.

The steady-state retention result of the change in eligibility ages to reflect Tier 2 benefits rules is presented in Figure 7.3. There is a negative effect on teacher retention through 27 years of teaching, implying that the delayed eligibility causes some individuals to exit teaching sooner. Retention declines more rapidly in years 1 to 10 and remains steadily lower through 27 years. There is no evidence that individuals delay exit from CPS during years 5 to 9 until the new vesting requirement at ten years of service, though it is possible that this effect is occurring but is being outweighed by other factors such as the sorting of teachers in the early career. As mentioned in Chapter Six in the discussion of our parameter estimates, sorting of teachers is the primary driver of early-career attrition; teachers with relatively low nonpecuniary taste for teaching leave CPS schools within the first ten years of service. Moving out the eligibility ages means that teachers with a low or marginal taste for teaching have less to gain from staying to vest.

Figure 7.3
Simulated Steady-State Retention Effects of
an Increase in Vesting and Eligibility Ages

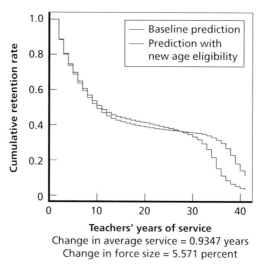

Teachers' years of service
Change in average service = 0.9347 years
Change in force size = 5.571 percent

RAND *RR1448-7.3*

The results in Figure 7.3 suggest that late-career decisionmaking appears to exhibit a lock-in effect, whereby teachers who stay for 20 years are highly likely to stay for 30 years. Because teachers with marginally lower taste have left, the average taste of teachers staying to 20 is higher than before. These teachers are willing to stay longer, as seen by higher retention from year 28 onward. The reason for the extension of service is twofold: (1) the delay in the age at which individuals can first begin collecting their benefit encourages longer careers, and (2) the higher eligibility age means the teachers no longer forgo pension benefits if they choose to stay in teaching after the preexisting normal retirement ages. The aggregate effect is an overall increase in average years taught of 0.935 years. Following our previous calculation, this would amount to 552 fewer teachers who would need to have been hired at entry in order to achieve the same number of expected teacher-years taught for the 1992–2000 entry cohorts and 1992 incumbents.

Two additional policy changes that take effect with the Tier 2 pension are a decrease in the COLA from a fixed 3-percent rate to the minimum of 3 percent or one-half the inflation rate, and an increase in the number of years included in calculating the average of final pay, from four to eight years. In the DRM, we assumed inflation is 3 percent in the steady state, meaning that under the new rules, the real value of the pension benefit would decline by 1.5 percent per year after collection begins.

The effect of both of these policies is very small, since their impact is spread out over the benefit receipt period and, in the case of the COLA, is further delayed into the future. The simulated response to the decrease in the COLA is 0.1516 fewer years of work on average. This would amount to 98 more teachers who would need to have been hired at entry to achieve the same number of expected teacher-years at baseline. The simulated response to the increase from four to eight years used to compute the final average pay is a decrease of 0.06 years worked, on average. Thirty-eight more teachers would need to be hired at entry to achieve the same number of teacher-years as at baseline. In both of these scenarios, the effect is similar to that observed in Figure 7.3, where teachers are more likely to exit in their early and mid-career but work longer around normal retirement age because of the diminished incentive to leave.

Finally, we consider a policy not part of the reforms affecting post-2010 hires: a decrease in the retirement benefit multiplier from 2.2 to 1 percent. At baseline, the retirement benefit of a teacher retiring at a normal retirement age is equal to the multiplier times years of service times the average of the best four years of pay. With Tier 1 benefits, the product of the multiplier and years of service cannot exceed 0.75. We consider the retention effect of a decrease in the multiplier from 2.2 to 1 percent.

The effect of this change on teacher retention is large: a decrease of 0.9141 in average years taught and a 5.448-percent decrease in work-years relative to baseline. However, the average change masks heterogeneity in the impact of the reform. As shown in the simulation results in Figure 7.4, many teachers exit teaching sooner, and retention is considerably lower by ten years of service. Retention then declines apace with baseline retention to 30 years of service. From then on, retention under the lower multiplier is higher than baseline retention. Teachers reach-

Figure 7.4
Simulated Steady-State Retention Effects of
a Decrease in the Pension Multiplier from
2.2 to 1 Percent

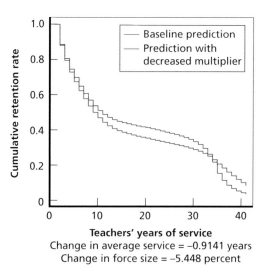

Change in average service = –0.9141 years
Change in force size = –5.448 percent

RAND *RR1448-7.4*

ing 34 years of service stay in teaching longer because the decrease in the retirement benefit decreases the incentive to leave (less money is forgone if the teacher stays). Also, the teachers reaching 34 years have a higher taste than those at baseline; teachers with a lower taste tended to leave in the first ten years. Thus, the policy change shortens the CPS careers of younger teachers who have learned the ropes and gained effectiveness in their first few years, and lengthens the CPS careers of older teachers with the highest taste for teaching in CPS. We caution, though, that having a high taste for teaching is not synonymous with being a highly effective teacher. The possibly differential effect of the policy change on teacher retention by teacher quality is not addressed here. Brown (2013b) found that when a policy change in retirement allowed teachers to retire early, less-effective teachers were more likely to take the offer, while more effective teachers stayed, as evidenced by an increase in standardized test scores after the policy took effect.

In contrast, we see that cutting the multiplier from 2.2 to 1 percent induces greater early sorting, with more lower-taste teachers leaving while higher-taste teachers stay for longer careers. Under this policy, a district might want to invest further in developing and supporting teacher effectiveness among those present after ten years of service.

Changes in deferred compensation are capable of having a large impact on teacher experience mix, based on our counterfactual experiments. In many ways, what we have presented represents the extreme cases of policy change: a sharp cut in benefits by decreasing the multiplier or a large increase in the age at which benefit can be collected. What we observed was that these large policy changes have a substantial influence on the decision to remain a career teacher, with most teachers who remain doing so because of their higher nonpecuniary returns from teaching. Alternatively, policy changes that are smaller in scope and more deferred, such as a change in COLA or a change in the number of years used to calculate final pay, have a smaller effect on retention.

The Combined Effect of Pension Reforms for Teachers Hired After 2010

We now simulate the combined effect of

1. an increase in the vesting, early claiming, and full benefit retirement age
2. a decrease in COLA from 3 percent to the minimum of 3 percent or one-half the inflation rate
3. basing the pension formula on the average of the highest eight years instead of the highest four years.

The simulation results for the combined policy changes appear in Figure 7.5. Average years of service increase by 0.604 years; this means that the same number of teacher work-years could be provided if the entry cohort had 377 fewer teachers. The extension of the claiming age is the primary influence, encouraging teachers to work longer than

**Figure 7.5
Simulated Steady-State Retention Effects of
the Pension Reforms for Teachers Hired
After 2010**

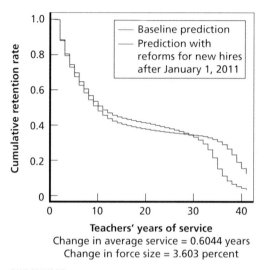

Teachers' years of service
Change in average service = 0.6044 years
Change in force size = 3.603 percent

would otherwise have been expected. Overall, the pension reforms decrease early-career retention but prolong the careers of teachers staying beyond ten years of service. The increase in retention after 34 years is relatively large, suggesting that the education leadership should consider whether incentives and supporting programs for these most senior teachers are appropriate or should be modified.

Conclusion

We successfully used the DRM to simulate the retention profiles of Chicago teachers under several hypothetical reforms to current and deferred compensation. The simulations suggest that although nonpecuniary benefits from teaching affect retention decisions (Chapter Six), current and deferred compensation are important levers for shaping the size and composition of the teaching workforce. Of the compensation changes we considered here, teacher retention was most negatively affected by the 3-percent salary reduction and decrease in the pension multiplier. Both policies cause a decrease in the financial return to working each year and lower lifetime earnings for teaching relative to outside employment options. As a result, early-career attrition increases. However, a $10,000 continuation bonus after five years of service did not have a large effect on early-career retention. This is an important finding, as retention bonuses have been used effectively in the military, and this type of compensation is more amenable to targeted retention than across-the-board changes to salary or retirement benefits.

CHAPTER EIGHT

Conclusion

In this study we estimated a structural model of the retention decisions of teachers in CPS. In the model, rational, forward-looking teachers make retention decisions each year over their career with CPS. The key factors that may be related to retention and are included in the model are current and expected salary earnings, future pension income, external wage opportunities, and preference for teaching in CPS relative to other professional options.

Overall, a fairly streamlined model that included both a permanent taste component and a depreciating early-career taste component nicely fit teacher retention over the entire career. The estimates indicate that teachers find a significant nonpecuniary benefit to teaching, and this benefit varies widely by individual and years of service. The mean taste for teaching early in the career is on par with the starting salary. Its mean value evolves over the career yet is positive in all years, providing a buffer against negative shocks. Simulations also indicate an important role for current and deferred compensation. Teacher retention throughout the career profile was sensitive to salary reduction. However, a $10,000 continuation bonus after five years of service was not sufficient to swamp the importance of taste or to have a large effect on early-career retention. In terms of deferred compensation, policies that cut the pension multiplier in half and that increased the pension normal retirement age had the largest effect on retention, reducing retention substantially through the mid-career but causing higher retention rates after 30 years of service.

Given that our research is the first to apply the structural stochastic dynamic programming modeling approach to modeling teacher retention, we highlight the findings that may be applicable to modeling teacher retirement in other settings. First, it was essential to estimate the DRM with data in which teacher retention behavior could be observed over the entire career profile. Although we had a long panel of teachers available (1979–2012), it was not long enough to observe even the earliest cohorts becoming eligible for retirement benefits. When the 1979–2000 entry cohorts were used to estimate the DRM, the predicted retention profile fit the observed retention profile well early in the career but did not capture the discrete drops in retention at retirement eligibility, where the pension financial incentives are particularly strong. This problem was addressed by modifying the model to accommodate both incumbent teachers (those who began teaching before 1979) and entry cohorts. With this approach, we were able to fit the full retention profile well using only ten years of panel data—observed retention behavior from 1992–2012 for incumbents present in 1992 and entry cohorts 1992–2000. With this modification, the DRM model provides the option to study retention across the service profile in contexts where long panel data are not available.

Second, we found that model fit depended on the presence of an early-career taste factor. The predicted retention profile using the estimates from a model that included only a permanent component of taste for teaching in CPS suggested that taste for teaching evolved with experience and, in particular, had a temporarily high value in the initial years of teaching. To address this, we included a depreciating early-career taste component. This specification provided the best fit of the retention profile across the career. While the empirical analysis suggests that teachers have an inflated likelihood of remaining in teaching early in their careers, it does not supply the cause, and there is little in the literature to explain this apparent reduction in the nonpecuniary rewards from teaching over the first decade of a teacher's career. Future applications of DRM in other settings will test the robustness of this result; however, this finding suggests a place for research that focuses on teachers' expectations as they enter teaching, their learning over the early-career years, and changes to working conditions and responsibilities over the career that affect retention.

There are several avenues for future research that build on the flexible baseline DRM for teacher retention developed here. The research could be extended to include Illinois teachers in other districts in addition to Chicago. It might be the case that early-career taste for teaching influences where teachers eventually locate and whether they stay in teaching. Extending the model to use the entire sample of teachers poses some challenges. For example, while CTPF is similar to the Illinois Teachers Pension Fund, they are managed by separate entities and have minor differences in benefit rules that must be taken into account. The extended model would also have to account for variation in pay by district and allow movement between districts, including movement (switching) costs. It would also be attractive to find instances of quasi-experimental variation that could offer a greater range of policy variation as the model seeks to identify the underlying parameters.

While we used the estimated model to simulate the effect of several policy changes, including an actual change in Chicago teachers' pension, we did not provide any estimates of the effect of these changes on compensation costs or pension liabilities. Teachers' defined benefit retirement plans are underfunded in nearly all states, and the political pressure to reduce the pension burden on state and local budgets continues to increase. Extending our analysis to estimate the change in pension liabilities associated with proposed policy changes and to identify the pension reforms most efficient in terms of maintaining the teaching workforce for a given level of cost reduction is a top priority. We have recently done similar work on the analysis of possible reforms to the military retirement benefit system (Asch, Hosek, and Mattock, 2014; Asch, Mattock, and Hosek, 2015). These analyses showed, for example, the cost of changing the military system from a wholly defined benefit system to a blended system that retained the defined benefit but at a lower multiplier (2 percent instead of 2.5 percent) and added a defined contribution system that enabled many more service members to vest in at least some retirement benefit. The analyses showed the cost, and cost savings, of many variants of the reform compared with the existing system. The analysis also revealed that the reform would require the introduction of a mid-career continuation pay to sustain the baseline retention profile. With the addition of costing modules to the teacher dynamic retention model, we can leverage this capability to study policy options for educator pensions in Chicago, the state of Illinois, and in other states and cities. The DRM we estimated explicitly incorporates only the financial incentives to teach. Future work can enrich this model to incorporate characteristics of the school, changes in the work environment and responsibilities, and changes in student characteristics explicitly. For example, the estimates of the enriched model would allow us to simulate how changes to the size of the student body or education reforms that challenge teachers to adopt new methods will affect the retention of teachers. These estimates will enable a direct comparison of the importance of these specific nonpecuniary characteristics of the work environment to financial compensation over the career profile, which could assist human resource managers and policymakers in creating policies that address compensation, work conditions, or the school environment to efficiently target retention of teachers at struggling schools or at particular points in their careers. The notion of compensation could also be expanded to include health insurance as part of the retirement package, and the model could value it in terms of cost avoided to purchase similar insurance on the market.

Finally, in a time of large reforms to teacher compensation, especially teacher pensions, it is important to understand not only the effect of these policies on the number of teachers who leave at particular points in the career, but also on which teachers leave, to account for the total turnover costs due to policy changes. Our results indicate that taste for teaching is a significant driver of retention decisions and that there is large variance in the nonpecuniary rewards of teaching across the population. This implies that exits from teaching in response to policy changes will be highly selected, making the extent to which taste for teaching is correlated with teachers' skills for producing student achievement an important consideration. This is supported by a small literature that suggests that more-effective teachers are more likely to continue teaching in their schools or districts, and that less-effective teachers are more likely to exit in response to increases in the value of their accumulated retirement benefits. In addition, sufficient supply of effective teachers across subject areas is necessary to promote learning. An extension of our model will allow us to test for differences in taste by teacher effectiveness, subject area taught (e.g., math and science), and other characteristics. Data permitting, the extended model will allow for differences in the mean as well as the standard deviation of taste. Incorporating teacher effectiveness into the DRM will allow us to see the extent to which alternative compensation structures are proselective, or not, on quality and to simulate the effect of compensation changes on student achievement. This advancement will require additional panel data on student test scores, but we consider this an essential next step in this research agenda.

Selected CTPF Provisions

Reforms of CTPF Retirement Benefits

CTPF Before 1998

A legislated reform set the pension multiplier at 2.2 percent for all creditable service accrued after July 1, 1998. Prior to this reform, the CTPF multiplier (M) had a stepped schedule with multiplier values of 1.67 – 2.3 percent depending on years of service (Table 2.1). This change increased the generosity of the pension benefits substantially. A teacher who had earned all of her service under the pre-1998 formula and retired at age 60 with 20 years of service would receive a pension benefit of 35.7 percent (1.67 percent × 10 + 1.9 percent × 10) of final average salary. If she had earned all years of service under the post-1998 formula, she would receive a benefit of 44 percent (20 × 2.2 percent) of final average salary. The employee contribution rate also increased to cover the more generous benefits, but the structure of the benefit calculation and other pension features were unchanged. The 2.2-percent multiplier applies to all service earned after 1998, regardless of when a teacher was hired. However, when a teacher's pension benefits are calculated at retirement, service earned prior to July 1, 1998, enters the benefit calculation under the prereform formula unless the teacher has paid an additional fee to upgrade all service to the 2.2-percent formula (detailed below in this appendix). The example in Table 2.2 assumes the 2.2-percent formula is applicable.

2011 Pension Reform

Legislation passed in 2010 introduced a second tier to CTPF. Teachers who became members of CTPF on or after January 1, 2011, became members in Tier 2. Tier 2, like Tier 1, is a defined benefit pension plan. The structure of benefit calculation is also identical to Tier 1, and the benefit multiplier is also 2.2 percent. However, several other changes to the pension rules, summarized in Table 2.2, substantially reduced the generosity of the retirement program. The service requirement for vesting was increased from five to ten years, excluding teachers with shorter careers in Chicago from any benefits. Approximately 50 percent of CPS teachers leave before completing ten years of service. The full benefits retirement age increased to 67 years old with ten years of service. This change required teachers to delay retirement by a minimum of five years relative to Tier 1 to receive the same annual benefit, effectively cutting lifetime retirement benefits. A lengthening of the window for the calculation of the FAS from four to eight years decreased the annual benefit amount for most teachers. Finally, a reduction in the cost of living adjustment of benefits postretirement also reduced expected pension wealth.

Upgrading Service Earned Prior to July 1, 1998

Teachers who were active contributors to CTPF on July 1, 1998, or who worked for at least one year after the July 1, 1998, pension reform are allowed to "upgrade" their prereform service credits to the 2.2-percent formula with an additional payment. The teacher must upgrade all service prior to the reform or none of it; partial upgrades are not allowed.

The cost to purchase the upgrade for each year of service is 1 percent of the teacher's highest annual salary in the four years prior to the year in which the teacher applied for the upgrade. The cost is capped at 20 years of service for all teachers who earned more than 20 years of service credit before July 1, 1998. For instance, a teacher wanting to upgrade 10 years of service and with a salary of $68,000 would need to pay $6,800. This fee may be paid directly by personal check, with tax-deferred rollover funds from a qualified retirement account, through payroll deductions distributed over five years, or through deductions from the first 24 pension payments. The cost of the upgrade is reduced by one year for every three years of service credit earned after July 1, 1998. Seventy to 80 percent of eligible teachers chose to purchase the upgrade (Fitzpatrick, 2015).

Early Retirement Without Reduction Option

Retirement benefits are reduced if a teacher retires "early," before reaching the full benefits age. In most cases, the reduction is based on the difference between the teacher's age and age 60. For example, a teacher with 20 years of service who retires and claims retirement benefits at age 59 would have her retirement benefit reduced by 6 percent, so that her early retirement benefit would be 0.94 times the full benefit amount. However, a high-service teacher who retires three years sooner, at age 56, with 32.95 years of service would also have her benefits reduced by only 6 percent because, although she is four years from age 60, she is only one year from meeting the 33.95 years of service threshold, at which point she would be eligible for the full retirement benefit.

This early retirement benefit reduction can be avoided by paying a fee. The teacher must pay 7 percent of salary for each year short of the normal retirement age. The district is also required to pay 20 percent of the teacher's salary for any teacher who elects the early retirement without reduction option.

Service Purchase Options

Approved, Unpaid Leave (Including Maternity/Paternity)

CTPF allows teachers to buy service for approved, unpaid leaves of absence. Typically, teachers must pay the contribution they would have made if they were working as well as any employer contributions. The cost is based on the salary and contributions in effect at the time of the leave, not the time of application. Interest on the total cost is 5 percent compounded annually beginning one year after termination of the leave. This purchase can be paid directly in a lump sum or by installments, and tax-deferred rollover funds from a qualified retirement account may be used. The maximum amount of service credit that can be purchased is 36 months for those who contributed after June 28, 2002, and 12 months for those who did not.

Public Elementary or High School Teaching

Teachers who were state certified teachers in Illinois, another state, or in a school operated by the U.S. government may purchase service credit. The cost is the same as for approved, unpaid leave. Teachers may purchase up to ten years; however, at the time of retirement, 60 percent of creditable service must have been earned in Chicago public schools or charter schools. Further, teachers must have withdrawn their contributions from the retirement system under which their previous service was earned.

Conversion of Unused Sick Leave

Unused sick leave can be converted to service credits. The amount that can be converted is currently capped at 244 days, equivalent to 1.4 years of service.

Teacher Years of Service, Teacher and Nonteacher Earnings Profiles, and Social Security

Teacher Years of Service Calculations and Exit Determinations

To address possible measurement error in the data, we assume that each year a full-time teacher is observed in the data is a creditable year of service for the purposes of the pension calculation. We do this rather than relying on the years of service reported in the administrative data. Service as measured by observed years as a teacher in the data is highly correlated with the reported service.[1] In addition, we assume that a one-year teacher absence from the data followed by a return within one year was not an actual absence if accrued service as reported in the administrative data incremented by two years. For example, consider a teacher observed in 2006 and 2008, but not in 2007. If her service is five years at the end of 2006 and seven years at the end of 2008, we assume that she was actually teaching in 2007 but was not reflected in the roster due to administrative error. However, if her service is five years at the end of 2006 and six years at the end of 2008, we treat this as a real temporary absence.

---

[1]   Using the ISBE data, we sorted by fiscal year and person identifier and generated a count of the number of times the individual was observed in the ISBE data, such that count increased monotonically with time. For CPS teachers, the correlation between the generated count and the years of reported state experience was 0.74.

The leave policy for tenured teachers in the CPS system is fairly generous. Teachers may be granted up to four years of approved unpaid leave for each new child (by birth or adoption) and up to eight years of consecutive leave. For leaves of less than one year, the teacher can return to her previous position. After one year, the teacher is no longer guaranteed the same position but maintains priority for placement. About a quarter (27 percent) of teachers in the Chicago 1992 to 2000 entry cohorts, followed to 2012, had a gap in service.

The data do not identify whether a teacher absent from the data in a given year was on an approved leave or had the intention of returning to teaching in Chicago. To handle this in the estimation, we assume that teachers who return to work in Chicago within two years of exit were on an approved temporary leave and intended to return to teaching. They are retained in the sample, and their years of creditable service are calculated as the actual observed years teaching. The two-year window captures 71 percent of observed returns. A longer window would have captured a higher percentage but increased the chance of including teachers who left the CPS without an approved absence and for reasons such as employment in a different job or raising young children. Such absences are relevant but not pursued in the current version of the retention model.[2]

Chicago Teacher Earnings Profile

Teacher pay tables typically follow a linear growth path with changes in the growth rate at certain milestones of service. Consequently, we use a piecewise linear specification for earnings, where the years of service variables for each piece depend on the individual teacher's observed years of service. $YoS_a(YoS)$, $a = 1,\ldots, K$ represents K variables to be created and k_a, $a = 1,\ldots, K-1$ are the corresponding knots in the specification such that

$$YoS_a(YoS_i) = YoS_i \ if \ a = 1$$
$$YoS_a(YoS_i) = \max(0, \ YoS_i - k_{a-1}) \ if \ a = 2 \ldots K.$$

---

[2] An expanded version of the model could allow for longer absences and returns.

We include knots at 5, 10, 15, 20, and 25 years of service. We also include additional knots at 14, 19, and 24 years of service to capture discontinuous jumps in earnings at 15, 20, and 25 years of service that have occasionally been a component of CPS's teacher pay tables.

Using Teacher Service Record data for Chicago, we estimate a standard OLS regression, conditional on fiscal year, for full-time equivalent teachers employed for 9 or 10 months in the Chicago Public School District with between 0 and 35 years of service:

$$Salary_i = \beta_{intercept} + \beta_{\alpha=1} YoS_{a=1} + \beta_2 YoS_2 + \ldots + \beta_K YoS_K$$
$$+ (\beta_{M,A,1} YoS_1 + \beta_{M,A,2} YoS_2 + \ldots + \beta_{M,A,K} YoS_K) \times MA_i + \varepsilon_i.$$

The subscript MA_i is an indicator variable taking a value of 1 if the individual holds a master's degree.

The model is estimated separately by year. The r-squared measure is always above 0.50, and above 0.70 in 90 percent of the fiscal years, indicating that degree and years of service determine the majority of teachers' earnings profiles. Figure B.1 provides an example of the model's fit to the data. In our retention model estimation, we assume the teacher has a bachelor's degree rather than a master's.

Nonteacher Earnings Profile

We use an upper-censored Tobit model to estimate nonteacher earnings in the Chicago metropolitan area. For the specification $\mathbf{y} = \mathbf{X}\boldsymbol{\beta} + \boldsymbol{\varepsilon}$, where $\mathbf{y}$ represents continuous outcomes and the error is normally distributed and independent across observations, $\varepsilon \sim N(0, \sigma^2 \mathbf{I})$. We observe individual i's log earnings, y_i, for observations $i \in C$. Observations $i \in \mathcal{R}$ are right-censored; we know only that they are greater than or equal to the known threshold $y_{\mathcal{R}i}$. The log likelihood is

$$\ln L = -\frac{1}{2} \sum_{i \in C} w_i \left\{ \left(\frac{y_i - X_i \beta}{\sigma} \right)^2 + log 2\pi\sigma^2 \right\} + \sum_{i \in \mathcal{R}} w_i \log \left\{ 1 - \Phi \left(\frac{y_{\mathcal{R}i} - X_i \beta}{\sigma} \right) \right\},$$

where $\Phi()$ is the standard cumulative normal and w_i is the weight for the ith observation.

Figure B.1
Internal Earnings Profiles for Chicago Teachers, by Service and Education

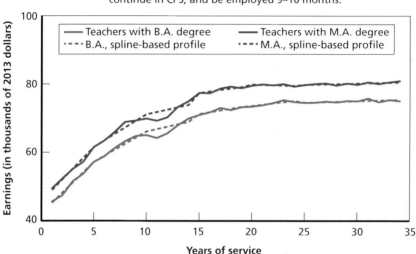

FY 1998 earnings by degree for teachers. Teachers must be full time, continue in CPS, and be employed 9–10 months.

Legend:
— Teachers with B.A. degree
---- B.A., spline-based profile
— Teachers with M.A. degree
---- M.A., spline-based profile

y-axis: Earnings (in thousands of 2013 dollars)
x-axis: Years of service

NOTE: Sample sizes: B.A. degree YoS(1–5): 3,498, YoS(6–10): 1,481, YoS(11–15): 498, YoS(16–20): 483, YoS(20–25): 1,072, YoS(26–30): 1,082, YoS(31–34): 350. M.A. degree YoS(1–5): 1,156, YoS(6–10): 1,000, YoS(11–15): 451, YoS(16–20): 514, YoS(20–25): 1,337, YoS(26–30): 1,563, YoS(31–34): 802.
RAND RR1448-B.1

Each individual i is designated as belonging to a cohort defined by birth year; a member of cohort c was born in years $c \in [c-2, c+2]$. We define cohorts in five-year intervals, namely, 1943, 1948,…,1978, 1983, and set 1963 as the baseline cohort.

We again use a piecewise linear specification, but in this case the knots depend on age rather than years of service. $Age_a(age_i)$, $a = 1,…,K$ represents K variables to be created and k_a, $a = 1,…, K{-}1$ are the corresponding knots. We set knots at five-year age groups between 22 and 65, though with the first age group being three years, 22 to 24, and the last age group being six years, 60 to 65. The omitted group is a male in the 1963 cohort with a B.A. degree (sample is restricted to BA+) who is not a veteran and who lives in a nonmetro area:

$$Age_a() = age_i \quad if\ a = 1$$
$$Age_a() = \max(0,\ age_i - k_{a-1}) \quad if\ a = 2 … K.$$

The explanatory variables include the age piecewise linear specification and indicator variables for female, college degree, graduate degree (more than four years of college), veteran, metro area, and Chicago metro area. The baseline regression specification for the 1963 cohort includes these variables, and the specifications for the other cohorts include the same variables but interacted with an indicator variable identifying the cohort. Year fixed effects are also included:

$$\beta_{intercept} + \beta_{a=1}Age_{a=1}() + \beta_2Age_2() + ... + \beta_K Age_K() + \beta_{female}\,female_i$$
$$+\beta_{CLG}college\,degree_i + \beta_{GRD}graduate\,degree_i + \beta_{VET}veteran_i$$
$$+\beta_{METRO}metro\,area_i + \beta_{CHICAGO}Chicago\,metro\,area_i$$
$$+ \sum_{\substack{c\in\{COHORTS\}\\c\neq baseline\ cohort}} Cohort_i$$

$$\times \left\{ \begin{array}{l} \beta_{c,intercept} + \beta_{c,a=1}Age_{a=1}() + \beta_{c,2}Age_2() + ... + \beta_{c,K}Age_K() \\ \beta_{c,female}female_i + \beta_{c,CLG}college\,degree_i + \beta_{c,GRD}graduate\,degree_i \\ +\beta_{c,VET}veteran_i + \beta_{c,METRO}metro\,area_i \\ +\beta_{c,CHICAGO}Chicago\,metro\,area_i \end{array} \right\}$$

$$+ \sum_{\substack{y=[1964,2014]\\y\neq 2011}}^{\square} \{\beta_y I[year_i = y]\}.$$

The age-earnings profile for a male in the 1963 cohort with a B.A. degree, who is not a veteran, who lives in a nonmetro area, and faces 2011 aggregate conditions is determined by

$$y_{c=1963} = \left\{ \begin{array}{l} \beta_{intercept} + \beta_{a=1}Age_{a=1} \quad age_i \in [22,24] \\ \beta_{intercept} + \beta_{a=1}Age_{a=1} + \beta_2Age_2 \quad age_i \in [25,29] \\ \qquad\qquad \vdots \qquad \vdots \\ \beta_{intercept} + \beta_{a=1}Age_{a=1} + \beta_2Age_2 + ... + \beta_9Age_9 \quad age_i \in [60,65] \end{array} \right\}.$$

For nonbaseline cohorts, it is determined by

$$y_{c\neq1963} = \begin{cases} y_{c=1963} + \beta_{c,intercept} + \beta_{c,a=1}Age_{a=1} \; age_i \in [22,24] \\ y_{c=1963} + \beta_{c,intercept} + \beta_{c,a=1}Age_{a=1} + \beta_{c,2}Age_2 \; age_i \in [25,29] \\ \vdots \quad \vdots \\ y_{c=1963} + \beta_{c,intercept} + \beta_{c,a=1}Age_{a=1} + \beta_{c,2}Age_2 \\ +...+\beta_{c,9}Age_9 \; age_i \in [60,65] \end{cases}.$$

The marginal effect of age for the 1963 baseline cohort is

$$\frac{dy_{c=1963}}{dage} = \begin{cases} \beta_{a=1} \; age_i \in [22,24] \\ \beta_{a=1} + \beta_{a=2} \; age_i \in [25,29] \\ \vdots \quad \vdots \\ \beta_{a=1} + \beta_{a=2} +...+ \beta_{a=9} \; age_i \in [60,65] \end{cases},$$

and the marginal effect of age for nonbaseline cohorts c is

$$\frac{dy_{c\neq1963}}{dage} = \begin{cases} \left(\beta_{a=1} + \beta_{c,a=1}\right) age_i \in [22,24] \\ \left(\beta_{a=1} + \beta_{c,a=1}\right) + \left(\beta_{a=2} + \beta_{c,a=2}\right) age_i \in [25,29] \\ \vdots \quad \vdots \\ \left(\beta_{a=1} + \beta_{c,a=1}\right) + \left(\beta_{a=2} + \beta_{c,a=2}\right) \\ +...+ \left(\beta_{a=9} + \beta_{c,a=9}\right) age_i \in [60,65] \end{cases}.$$

The cohort earnings profiles were then simulated using the model estimates. We assumed the following variable values:

- Year = 2013[3]
- Education = College Graduate, but no Graduate Degree
- Is a Veteran = No
- Gender = Male

---

[3]   An alternative way of simulating the earnings profiles would be to not fix the year to 2013, thus allowing the cohorts to experience aggregate market shocks as they happen. This would, of course, require us to assume in the model that they fully anticipated these shocks.

- Living in a metro area = Yes
- Living in the Chicago Metro Area = Yes.

Social Security

Teaching positions in CPS are not covered by Social Security. However, a teacher's choices about whether and when to discontinue teaching in Chicago can affect her eligibility for Social Security benefits and the size of those benefits, should she work in a covered job after teaching. Because Chicago teachers do not contribute to Social Security, years worked and wages earned while teaching in CPS are excluded when determining Social Security eligibility and calculating lifetime average earnings that enter the Social Security benefit formula. In addition, a Social Security rule called the windfall elimination provision reduces a teacher's Social Security benefits based on her own earnings record outside of CPS if she has less than 30 years of earnings in Social Security covered employment. This effect of teaching in Chicago versus alternative employment on expected future Social Security benefits was incorporated into one version of the DRM estimation; however, this did not improve the model fit. As a consequence, our preferred specification, which was used for policy simulations, excludes the Social Security–related incentives.

References

Aguirregabiria, Victor, and Pedro Mira, "Dynamic Discrete Choice Structural Models: A Survey," *Journal of Econometrics*, Vol. 156, No. 1, pp. 38–67, May 2010.

Asch, Beth J., James Hosek, and Michael G. Mattock, *Toward Meaningful Military Compensation Reform: Research in Support of DoD's Review*, Santa Monica, Calif.: RAND Corporation, RR-501-OSD, 2014. As of July 23, 2015:
http://www.rand.org/pubs/research_reports/RR501.html

Asch, Beth J., James Hosek, Michael G. Mattock, and Christina Panis, *Assessing Compensation Reform: Research in Support of the 10th Quadrennial Review of Military Compensation*, Santa Monica, Calif.: RAND Corporation, MG-764-OSD, 2008. As of March 29, 2016:
http://www.rand.org/pubs/monographs/MG764.html

Asch, Beth J., Michael G. Mattock, and James Hosek, *A New Tool for Assessing Workforce Management Policies over Time: Extending the Dynamic Retention Model*, Santa Monica, Calif.: RAND Corporation, RR-113-OSD, 2013. As of February 25, 2016:
http://www.rand.org/pubs/research_reports/RR113.html

———, *The Federal Civil Service Workforce: Assessing the Effects on Retention of Pay Freezes, Unpaid Furloughs, and Other Federal-Employee Compensation Changes in the Department of Defense*, Santa Monica, Calif.: RAND Corporation, RR-514-OSD, 2014a. As of July 23, 2015:
http://www.rand.org/pubs/research_reports/RR514.html

———, *How Do Federal Civilian Pay Freezes and Retirement Plan Changes Affect Employee Retention in the Department of Defense?* Santa Monica, Calif.: RAND Corporation, RR-678-OSD, 2014b. As of July 23, 2015:
http://www.rand.org/pubs/research_reports/RR678.html

———, *Reforming Military Retirement: Analysis in Support of the Military Compensation and Retirement Modernization Commission*, Santa Monica, Calif.: RAND Corporation, RR-1022-MCRMC, 2015. As of August 1, 2015:
http://www.rand.org/pubs/research_reports/RR1022.html

Bajari, Patrick, C. Lanier Benkard, and Jonathan Levin, "Estimating Dynamic Models of Imperfect Competition," *Econometrica*, Vol. 75, No. 5, September 2007, pp. 1331–1370.

Borkovsky, Ron, Ulrich Doraszelski, and Yaroslov Kryukov, "A Dynamic Quality Ladder Model with Entry and Exit: Exploring the Equilibrium Correspondence Using the Homotopy Method," Quantitative Marketing and Economics, Vol. 10, No. 2, 2012, pp. 197–229.

Boyd, Donald, Pamela Grossman, Marsha Ing, Hamilton Lankford, Susanna Loeb, and James Wyckoff, "The Influence of School Administrators on Teacher Retention Decisions," *American Educational Research Journal*, Vol. 48, No. 2, 2011, pp. 303–333.

Brown, Kristine M., "The Link Between Pensions and Retirement Timing: Lessons From California Teachers," *Journal of Public Economics*, Vol. 98, 2013a, pp. 1–14.

———, "Out with the Old: The Effect of Teacher Retirements on Student Outcomes," working paper, 2013b.

Chicago Alliance of Charter Teachers and Staff, "ACTS-Represented Schools," web page, Washington, D.C.: American Federation of Teachers, undated. As of August 19, 2015:
http://chicagoacts.org/local-4343/partner-campuses

Chicago Public Schools, "CPS Stats and Facts," web page, 2015a. As of August 19, 2015:
http://cps.edu/About_CPS/At-a-glance/Pages/Stats_and_facts.aspx

———, "Local School Council Historical Background," time line, 2015b. As of August 19, 2015:
http://cps.edu/Pages/LSCHistoricalbackground.aspx

Chicago Teachers' Pension Fund, "Your CTPF Pension," undated. As of February 2, 2016:
http://www.ctpf.org/active_members/tieredbenefit.pdf

Chicago Teachers Union, *CTU Contract*, undated(a). As of September 15, 2015:
http://contract.ctunet.com/article:0

———, *For Members: 2012–2015 Contract*, web portal, undated(b). As of August 19, 2015:
http://www.ctunet.com/for-members/final-contract-language

Chingos, Matthew M., and Martin R. West, "Do More Effective Teachers Earn More Outside the Classroom?" *Education Finance and Policy*, Vol. 7, No. 1, 2012, pp. 8–43. As of August 17, 2015:
http://www.mattchingos.com/cw_efp2012.pdf

Clark, Robert, "Evolution of Public-Sector Retirement Plans: Crisis, Challenges, and Change," *The Labor Lawyer*, Vol. 27, No. 2, 2012, pp. 257–273.

Coile, Courtney, and Jonathan Gruber, "Future Social Security Entitlements and the Retirement Decision," *Review of Economics and Statistics,* Vol. 89, No. 2, 2007, pp. 234–246.

Costrell, Robert, and Josh McGee, "Teacher Pension Incentives, Retirement Behavior, and Potential for Reform in Arkansas," *Education Finance and Policy,* Vol. 4, No. 2, 2010, pp. 492–518.

Costrell, Robert, and Michael Podgursky, "Peaks, Cliffs, and Valleys: The Peculiar Incentives in Teacher Retirement Systems and Their Consequences for School Staffing," *Education Finance and Policy,* Vol. 4, No. 2, 2009, pp. 175–211. As of February 24, 2016:
http://www.mitpressjournals.org/doi/abs/10.1162/edfp.2009.4.2.175#.Vs9GmVIryao

CTU—*See* Chicago Teachers Union.

de la Torre, Marisa, Elaine Allensworth, Sanja Jagesic, James Sebastian, Michael Salmonowicz, Coby Meyers and R. Dean Gerdeman, *Turning Around Low-Performing Schools in Chicago,* Chicago: University of Chicago Consortium on Chicago School Research, 2013.

de la Torre, Marisa, Molly F. Gordon, Paul Moore, Jennifer Cowhy, Sanja Jagesic, and Michelle H. Huynh, *School Closings in Chicago: Understanding Families' Choices and Constraints for New School Enrollment,* Chicago: University of Chicago Consortium on School Research, 2015.

Feng, Li, and Tim R. Sass, "Teacher Quality and Teacher Mobility," Andrew Young School of Policy Studies Research Paper Series, 12-08, 2012.

Fitzpatrick, Maria, "How Much Do Public School Teachers Value Their Pension Benefits?" *American Economic Journal: Economic Policy,* Vol. 7, No. 4, 2015, pp. 165–188.

Fitzpatrick, Maria, and Michael Lovenheim, "How Does Teacher Retirement Affect Student Achievement?" *American Economic Journal: Economic Policy,* Vol. 6, No. 3, 2014, pp. 120–154.

Furgeson, Joshua, Robert Strauss, and William Vogt, "The Effects of Defined Benefit Pension Incentives and Working Conditions on Teacher Retirement Decisions," *Education Finance and Policy,* Vol. 1, No. 3, 2006, pp. 316–348.

Goldhaber, Dan, Betheny Gross, and Daniel Player, "Teacher Career Paths, Teacher Quality, and Persistence in the Classroom: Are Public Schools Keeping Their Best?" *Journal of Policy Analysis and Management,* Vol. 30, No. 1, 2011, pp. 57–87.

Gotz, Glenn A., and John McCall, *A Dynamic Retention Model for Air Force Officers: Theory and Estimates,* Santa Monica, Calif.: RAND Corporation, R-3028-AF, 1984. As of March 27, 2013:
http://www.rand.org/pubs/reports/R3028.html

Hanushek, Eric A., John F. Kain, and Steven G. Rivkin, "Why Public Schools Lose Teachers," *Journal of Human Resources*, Vol. 39, No. 2, 2004, pp. 326–354.

Hendricks, Matthew D., "Towards an Optimal Teacher Salary Schedule: Designing Base Salary to Attract and Retain Effective Teachers," *Economics of Education Review*, Vol. 47, 2015, pp. 143–167.

Hotz, V. Joseph, and Robert A. Miller, "Conditional Choice Probabilities and the Estimation of Dynamic Models," *Review of Economic Studies*, Vol. 60, No. 3, July 1993, pp. 497–529.

Illinois State Board of Education, *Illinois State Report Card Data*, web portal, Springfield, Ill., undated. As of January 29, 2016:
http://www.isbe.net/assessment/report_card.htm

Ingersoll, Richard M., and Michael Strong, "The Impact of Induction and Mentoring Programs for Beginning Teachers: A Critical Review of the Research," *Review of Educational Research*, Vol. 81, No. 2, 2011, pp. 201–233. As of August 31, 2015:
http://rer.sagepub.com/content/81/2/201.full.pdf+html

Institute of Education Sciences, National Center for Education Statistics, *Common Core of Data: Search for Public School Districts*, database, U.S. Department of Education, undated. As of August 19, 2015:
http://nces.ed.gov/ccd/districtsearch/

ISBE—*See* Illinois State Board of Education.

Kapadia, Kavita, Vanessa Coca, and John Q. Easton, *Keeping New Teachers: A First Look as the Influences of Induction in the Chicago Public Schools*, Chicago: Consortium on School Research, 2007. As of August 31, 2015:
http://ccsr.uchicago.edu/sites/default/files/publications/keeping_new_teachers012407.pdf

Keane, Michael P., and Kenneth I. Wolpin, "The Career Decisions of Young Men," *Journal of Political Economy*, Vol. 105, No. 3, June 1997, pp. 473–522.

Koedel, Cory, Michael Podgursky, and Shishan Shi, "Teacher Pension Systems, the Composition of the Teaching Workforce, and Teacher Quality," *Journal of Policy Analysis and Management*, Vol. 32, No. 3, 2013, pp. 574–596.

Loeb, Susanna, Linda Darling-Hammond, and John Luczak, "How Teaching Conditions Predict Teacher Turnover in California Schools," *Peabody Journal of Education*, Vol. 80, No. 3, 2005, pp. 44–70. As of July 23, 2015:
http://dx.doi.org/10.1207/s15327930pje8003_4

Mansfield, Richard K., "Teacher Quality and Student Inequality," *Journal of Labor Economics*, Vol. 33, No. 3 (Part 1), July 2015, pp. 751–788.

Mattock, Michael G., and Jeremy Arkes, *The Dynamic Retention Model for Air Force Officers: New Estimates and Policy Simulations of the Aviator Continuation Pay Program*, Santa Monica, Calif.: RAND Corporation, TR-470-AF, 2007. As of March 27, 2013:
http://www.rand.org/pubs/technical_reports/TR470.html

Mattock, Michael G., James Hosek, and Beth J. Asch, *Reserve Participation and Cost Under a New Approach to Reserve Compensation*, Santa Monica, Calif.: RAND Corporation, MG-1153-OSD, 2012. As of March 27, 2013:
http://www.rand.org/pubs/monographs/MG1153.html

Munnell, Alicia H., and Jean-Pierre Aubry, *The Funding of State and Local Pensions: 2014–2018*, Issue Brief No. 45, Boston: Center for Retirement Research at Boston College, 2015. As of February 3, 2016:
http://crr.bc.edu/briefs/the-funding-of-state-and-local-pensions-2014-2018/

Murnane, Richard, and Randall Olsen, "The Effects of Salaries and Opportunity Costs on Length of Stay in Teaching: Evidence from North Carolina," *Journal of Human Resources*, Vol. 25, No. 1, 1990, pp. 106–124. As of July 23, 2015:
http://www.jstor.org/stable/145729

National Commission on Teaching and America's Future, *The High Cost of Teacher Turnover*, policy brief, Washington, D.C., 2007. As of July 23, 2015:
http://nctaf.org/wp-content/uploads/2012/01/NCTAF-Cost-of-Teacher-Turnover-2007-policy-brief.pdf

Ni, Shawn, and Michael Podgursky, "How Teachers Respond to Pension System Incentives: New Estimates and Policy Applications," University of Missouri Economics Working Paper 11-11, 2015.

Papay, John P., Andrew Bacher-Hicks, Lindsey C. Page, and William H. Marinell, "The Challenge of Teacher Retention in Urban Schools: Evidence of Variation from a Cross-Site Analysis," Social Science Electronic Publishing, May 2015. As of August 31, 2015:
http://ssrn.com/abstract=2607776

Ronfeldt, Matthew, Susanna Loeb, and James Wyckoff, "How Teacher Turnover Harms Student Achievement," *American Educational Research Journal*, Vol. 50, No. 1, 2013, pp. 4–36.

Rust, John, "Structural Estimation of Markof Decision Processes," in *Handbook of Econometrics, Volume 4*, R. F. Engle and D. L. McFadden, eds., Elsevier Science, 1994.

Smith, Thomas M., and Richard M. Ingersoll, "What Are the Effects of Induction and Mentoring on Beginning Teacher Turnover?" *American Educational Research Journal*, Vol. 41, No. 3, 2004, pp. 681–714. As of August 31, 2015:
http://aer.sagepub.com/content/41/3/681.full.pdf+html

Steele, Jennifer L., Matthew J. Pepper, Matthew G. Springer, and J. R. Lockwood, "The Distribution and Mobility of Effective Teachers: Evidence from a Large, Urban School District," *Economics of Education Review*, Vol. 48, 2015, pp. 86–101.

Stinebrickner, Todd R., "An Empirical Investigation of Teacher Attrition," *Economics of Education Review*, Vol. 17, No. 2, 1998, pp. 127–136.

Stock, James, and David Wise, "Pensions, the Option Value of Work, and Retirement," *Econometrica*, Vol. 58, No. 5, September 1990, pp. 1151–1180.

Teachers' Retirement System of the State of Illinois, *Tier I Member Guide, 2015*, 2015a. As of July 23, 2015:
http://trs.illinois.gov/members/pubs/tier1guide/guide.pdf

———, *Employer Guide*, State of Illinois, September 2015c. As of January 29, 2016:
https://trs.illinois.gov/employers/guide/guide.pdf

Van der Klaauw, Wilbert, "On the Use of Expectations Data in Estimating Structural Dynamic Choice Models," *Journal of Labor Economics*, Vol. 30, No. 3, July 2012, pp, 521–554.